Praise for *Intentional Parenting*

As educators and Christians, we bring all of our natural strengths, God-given assets, and distinct personalities into the classroom. However, along with these gifts, we carry our wounds, insecurities, and fears. Our unique persona manifests itself in the way we teach and engage students and surfaces in our approach to the different situations we encounter in the context of schools. When we deepen our intimacy with Christ, He redeems our character flaws and insecurities, freeing us to be a truer version of the individual He intended us to be. This refinement enhances our impact on our students and strengthens our ability to speak into their lives in authentic and significant ways. *Intentional Parenting* fully captures this complexity through the context of parenting. We parent who we are. This book equips parents at all stages and provides them with a principle-centered approach to parenting that challenges them to be reflective and proactive as they invest spiritually, emotionally, and physically in their children.

NATHANIEL H. MORROW
ASSISTANT HEADMASTER AND HIGH SCHOOL PRINCIPAL
CHRIST PRESBYTERIAN ACADEMY, NASHVILLE, TENNESSEE

Each day I see parents attempting to complete a day filled with activities for their children. They plan each portion down to the very minute. Sadly, parents are not planning how they can be intentional in casting vision for their children and help launch them into the next season of their life. Our culture is in desperate need of a generation of parents who are willing to sacrifice in a redemptive way and be strategic and intentional in the lives of their children. David, Sissy, and Melissa have provided a great resource for those parents who want to know what it means to be an intentional parent and how that fleshes out on a daily basis. I highly recommend that you read this book, take it to heart, and put it to practice today.

BRAXTON BRADY
CHAPLAIN AND DIRECTOR OF BUILDING BOYS AND MAKING MEN
PRESBYTERIAN DAY SCHOOL, MEMPHIS, TENNESSEE

Intentional Parenting is a breath of fresh air to the tired parent and an encouragement to the frustrated parent. Occasionally our parenting batteries need to be charged, and this book provides the right combination of helpful reminders and new ideas. It will be a welcome tool in the hands of any parent.

DAVE STONE
PASTOR AND AUTHOR OF THE *FAITHFUL FAMILIES* SERIES

Sissy, David, and Melissa have three of the finest reputations I know. Their impact on the lives of children and parents is truly unparalleled. As personal friends of mine, I can't think of three people whom I'd rather have speak into my life, or the life of every child I know. The words in this book not only spring from decades of counseling experience, but also from a biblical premise which makes this a must-read for anyone with children—or for those like me who simply love them.

KELLY MINTER
SPEAKER AND AUTHOR OF *NEHEMIAH: A HEART THAT CAN BREAK*

INTENTIONAL
PARENTING

INTENTIONAL PARENTING

Autopilot is for planes

SISSY GOFF, DAVID THOMAS,
AND MELISSA TREVATHAN

THOMAS NELSON
Since 1798

NASHVILLE   DALLAS   MEXICO CITY   RIO DE JANEIRO

Published in Nashville, Tennessee, by Thomas Nelson. Thomas Nelson is a registered trademark of Thomas Nelson, Inc.

Thomas Nelson, Inc, titles may be purchased in bulk for educational, business, fund-raising, or sales promotional use. For information, please e-mail SpecialMarkets@ ThomasNelson.com.

Scripture quotations marked ESV are from the English Standard Version. © 2001 by Crossway Bibles, a division of Good News Publishers.

Scripture quotations marked HCSB are from HOLMAN CHRISTIAN STANDARD BIBLE. © 1999, 2000, 2002, 2003 by Broadman and Holman Publishers. All rights reserved.

Scripture quotations marked MSG are from The Message by Eugene H. Peterson. © 1993, 1994, 1995, 1996, 2000. Used by permission of NavPress Publishing Group. All rights reserved.

Scripture quotations marked NIV are from THE HOLY BIBLE, NEW INTERNATIONAL VERSION®, NIV® Copyright © 1973, 1978, 1984, 2011 by Biblica, Inc.™ Used by permission. All rights reserved worldwide.

Scripture quotations marked NIV1984 are from The Holy Bible, New International Version®, NIV®. Copyright ©1973, 1978, 1984 by Biblica, Inc.™ Used by permission of Zondervan. All rights reserved worldwide. www.zondervan.com.

Scripture quotations marked NKJV are taken from the NEW KING JAMES VERSION. © 1982 by Thomas Nelson, Inc. Used by permission. All rights reserved.

Library of Congress Cataloging-in-Publication Data

Thomas, David, 1970-
 Intentional parenting / David Thomas, Sissy Goff, and Melissa Trevathan.
  pages cm
 Includes bibliographical references.
 ISBN 978-0-8499-6454-1 (trade paper)
 1. Parenting--Religious aspects--Christianity. 2. Parent and child--Religious aspects--Christianity. 3. Families--Religious life. I. Goff, Sissy, 1970- II. Trevathan, Melissa, 1950- III. Thomas, David, 1970- Being an intentional parent. IV. Title.
 BV4526.3.T44 2013
 248.8'45--dc23

                                    2012041519

Printed in the United States of America
HB 02.01.2019

To all the kids and parents we've had
the opportunity to walk alongside.

Contents

Introduction

"I REALLY LIKE YOUR BOOK IDEA, BUT I'D RATHER read about how to make *my child* be encouraging, balanced, and spiritual (rather than me)." The father who said these words approached us at a recent parenting conference. He was asking about our newest book we were writing, which happens to be the one in your hands. And he was echoing what many parents would say in response to a book called *Intentional Parenting*.

Another man and his wife recently came to Daystar Counseling Ministries, where we all work, for what we call a "parent consultation." (Parent consultations are for parents who have questions or concerns but aren't necessarily sure their children need to come in for counseling.) He and his wife sat down, looking more than a little weary.

"Our ten-year-old daughter is what you might call 'challenging.' She yells anytime we say no. She wants her way constantly and will fight until the walls are falling in to get it. We've taken her to two counselors and one occupational therapist. But, today, it's just us. I really think that we've just been trying to outsource our parenting. We wanted someone who would fix her and then hand her back. But I'm starting to think maybe we need help too. I know I get to the end of my rope and become angrier than I should with her. I'm thinking that if we could learn to be better parents, she wouldn't feel the need to act out as much at home."

The second father is the kind of parent we're seeing more and more in our offices. He's a father who is aware of his daughter's struggles but knows that they don't exist in a vacuum. He knows he's a part of the problem too. And he can be a part of the solution—maybe even one of the most important parts.

We recently tried to do the math. The three of us have been counseling more than seventy-five years combined. But David and Sissy always like to point out that most of those years are Melissa's. She's our boss. She started Daystar in 1985, after years working as a youth director and the head of spiritual life at a school in Nashville. David has been the director of boys' counseling at Daystar since 1995, and Sissy's been the director of girls' counseling since 1993.

Daystar, if you've never heard of us, is a counseling ministry in Nashville, Tennessee. We see kids ranging from about ages five to eighteen. We offer individual counseling, group counseling, and a summer camp for our kid called Camp Hopetown. Daystar is a different kind of counseling office. As a matter of fact, one of our favorite quotes is from a child in counseling who said, "I don't go to Daystar for counseling. I just go to talk about my problems." We have spiced tea brewing in the lobby, offices that look like living rooms, and three dogs that are three of the most important counselors on our staff. Melissa's Old English sheepdog is named Blueberry. David's yellow Lab is named Owen. And Sissy's little Havanese is named Lucy and is the boss of them all.

Daystar's vision is "As one life touches another through the process of softening, shaping, and strengthening, God's hand begins to move. He uses a place that is not perfect, but is committed to being a safe place, to remind each of us of who He has created us to be, and who we will one day become." When we speak at churches or schools across the country, we always say, in the beginning, it's not that we're experts. We just have the honor of sitting with kids of all ages, and their parents, on a daily basis. We get to learn from them and then reflect what we've learned back to you.

One thing we've learned recently is that today's parents are changing. They're much more like the man who wanted to be a different parent than the one who simply wanted to change his children. They're honest. They're more self-aware. And they're wanting to learn what it means to be intentional parents.

We have a good idea that you fall into the second category. You've picked up this book, after all. As counselors, we believe that today's children will be profoundly impacted by the change in today's parents. You are giving them a tremendous gift in your intentionality.

What we'd really like to do is sit down with you and hear about you and your child. We'd like to get you a cup of tea and invite you into each of our offices. They're pretty different, by the way. Melissa sits in a rocking chair and has an office that is filled with soothing yellows and blues and speaks of rest and refreshment. David's chair of choice is made of well-worn leather, and his office invokes feelings of safety and strength. Sissy's office is bright, with yellow and red plaids, and prints that speak of warmth and encouragement.

So, grab a chair. Pick an office and come in. We'll sit and talk about all that you are as a parent already, and all you can do to be the intentional parent God frees you to be.

1.

Being an Intentional Parent

YEARS AGO I (DAVID) HAD A CONVERSATION WITH a young man I'd known for several years. I had seen him for the first time as a junior in high school, and then throughout his senior year. He went away to college, and midway through the first semester, he called home to ask his mom if he could set up an appointment when home on break. She agreed, wondering what might be going on with him, but called to set up a time to meet.

It was good to reconnect with this young man, to talk about the transition from high school to college, and discuss living on his own for the first time. He was dealing with the normal challenges of being a college freshman at a big school and adjusting to this new stage of life.

Somewhere along the way, we ended up talking about his memory of being dropped off and saying good-bye to his parents. I asked him what he remembered about that moment (a significant moment for every college student); he paused and stared ahead as he was chasing down that memory.

"David, my dad cried harder that day than I've ever seen him cry in my life." This young man's face gave me so much information about that moment with his dad. It was obvious that, months later, he was still feeling the impact of that exchange. He went on to say, "My dad could barely speak . . . He just kept saying, 'I love you, over and over. He just kept saying 'I love you so much.'"

I let him sit with his dad's words for some time, and then I asked, "How was your mom in that time?" His face changed; he chuckled and shifted. "She kept saying things like, 'Don't forget the milk I put in your mini-fridge. It will spoil in a week or so.'"

He continued while mimicking her voice. "'And you'll need to keep track of your meal plan account online. You will run out of money, and then you'll be in the cafeteria and won't be able to purchase a thing to eat.'"

We laughed together briefl, and then he finished. "The time finally came for my parents to say a last good-bye. My dad pulled the car around back and he was still crying. He hugged me one last time, and then my mom hugged me. They both got in the car, but before they drove away, my mom rolled down her window and yelled, 'Don't drink. It is so dangerous!'"

With those final words, his parents pulled away. He started laughing again, which gave me permission to join him.

I know this young man's mother. She is a kind, thoughtful, well-intentioned mother. She responded in that moment the way we are all vulnerable to responding—out of fear.

You may be reading this book and thinking back to your own moment of dropping a child off for college. Or maybe you are about to do that for the first time. Maybe you are the parent of a two-year-old and the idea of that moment seems so far away that you can barely wrap your mind and heart around it. Wherever you are in the journey of parenting, you can likely identify with this mom in some way. You can remember a moment in your parenting where you parented more out of fear than anything else.

When the three of us speak across the country to groups of parents, Melissa speaks beautifully to parenting out of fear instead of parenting out of love. When we parent out of fear, our kids never get the best of us, the most of us, or even what they really need from us. Parenting out of fear is a *reactive* form of parenting.

We'd love to invite you into more *proactive* parenting—thoughtful, intentional, strategic, and wise parenting. Or more *active* parenting—responsive, engaged, invested, connected parenting. It's difficult to parent out of love when we are simply reacting to everything going on around us. We are postured to *react* rather than *respond*.

I believe this college-aged boy's father was a beautiful picture of responding rather than reacting. He was responding to how much he loved this boy. He was responding to how much he is going to miss him. He was responding to the reality that he was closing a chapter on parenting this young man. He was responding to the emotions he felt when he looked at him and when he thought about the years he spent holding him and teaching him to catch a ball, ride a bike, memorize multiplication facts, shave, drive a car, tie a necktie, and ask a girl to dance. He was responding in love, and in turn parenting out of love.

We always have options. Sometimes we choose fear over

love. Sometimes we choose love over fear. You will continue to hear us invite you to extend grace to yourself in the journey of parenting. You are going to make mistakes. God can redeem the mistakes we make in parenting. He extends grace to us so that we can then extend grace and mercy to our children. Receive the grace and mercy that is available to you. And then do that thing we teach our kids to do when they fall off their bikes while learning to ride: get back up, dust yourself off, and try again.

Being an intentional parent means I get back on the bike and learn from the mistake I made last time around. Maybe I rode too close to the curb; maybe I didn't brake soon enough or didn't have a firm grip on the handlebars. Try doing it a little different next time around. If you need to take a break for a while, that's Okay. We all need breaks. A chance to stop, breathe, gain some perspective, and then we're more ready to try again.

Reconsider the Purpose

In Ezekiel 20:22 God spoke about the Israelites, saying, "I seriously considered dumping my anger on them, right there in the desert. But I thought better of it and acted out of *who I was*, not by *what I felt*, so that I might be honored and not blasphemed by the nations who had seen me bring them out" (MSG, emphasis added).

Those words resonate with me. I can't keep track of how many moments I've seriously considered dumping my anger. Or worse yet, the times I've gone ahead and just done it. I've walked in at the end of a long day to find the kitchen sink is still full of dinner's dirty dishes, no one let the dog out, wet towels line the bathroom floor, sports equipment and cleats are scattered throughout the house, and everyone's acting like the chore chart on the fridge is a recommendation more than a requirement.

Or there is arguing from the backseat of the car or the upstairs of the house, and my kids are acting more as if they are opposing teammates than members of the same family. The normal, daily moments of parenting take us to the ends of ourselves, and we respond less out of who we are and more out of what we feel. Being an intentional parent simply means I'm *growing* toward responding more out of who I am, who God made me to be, than out of how I feel.

Why did you decide to become a parent?

I enjoy asking parents this question. I mostly enjoy watching people's faces in response to the question. Most often they just stare at me as if maybe I'd asked something like, "Why did you decide to buy a car?" or "Why do you go to the grocery each week?" I hear a range of responses like:

- "I never really thought about the why."
- "It seemed like the next natural step."
- "I always knew that I wanted to be a mom."
- "I saw myself as a parent. It just felt like the right thing to do."
- "I can't really describe it, I just knew it was time."

I then give permission to not have an answer to the question. I don't think it's one most of us gave much consideration to. I was twenty-three when I asked my wife to marry me, and we

married the following year. Most developmental theorists agree
that adolescence ends for males around twenty-three to twenty-
four. So I was still finishing adolescence when we married, and
I was certainly not thinking about the next decisions in life with
a lot of maturity or wisdom. I, like many dads, stumbled into
parenting because it was just what you did next. I never *really*
considered the purpose.

I certainly never considered what parenting would do *to* me,
in me, and *through* me. Decades later, I am just beginning to
wrap my mind around that. I suspect I'll still be figuring that
out until I'm done. I only know this much so far: As I reread
the Genesis narrative, I see important insight into the parenting
journey. As we trace back through the Creation story, we understand God created man and woman in His image, charged them
to multiply and be fruitful, and blessed the first birth. Genesis
4 is all about parenting. It begins with Adam and Eve giving
birth to a son, then another son, one killing the other, and then
giving birth to a third son, Seth. The story of parenting evolves
into the next generation as Seth and his wife give birth to a son
named Enosh.

The fourth chapter of Genesis closes with these last words,
which I believe speak to all of us about the purpose of parenting.
They are, "At that time people began to call on the name of the
LORD" (Gen. 4:26 NIV).

We are reminded within those words that parenting will
take us to the end of ourselves. It will drive us to a place of
dependence, of crying out for help, of leaning into God for wisdom and strength. We aren't designed to do this on our own.
We need God.

Prepare for Disruption

The words of Genesis speak not only to dependence but also to disruption. Without much difficulty, we can identify with some of the emotions Adam and Eve experienced in stepping into the journey of parenting for the first time. Can you think back to the first time you saw the face of your son or daughter? Perhaps that introduction happened in a hospital room as a doctor or nurse placed this new life into your arms for the first time. Or maybe you were thousands of miles away from home, in an orphanage, and caretakers entered the room, carrying a child you had only seen in photographs up to that moment. Do you remember how something shifted in you? Do you remember how you felt something stir in you that you had never experienced before?

A transformation was taking place. You entered the room one person and you left the room a different one. Something shifted in you. A deeper place was carved out in you—the capacity for something more.

I can still remember seeing my firstborn for the first time. Watching my wife struggle in childbirth, life coming from her, seeing this beautiful little girl and being overtaken with emotion. It wrecked me. I could not contain what was inside of me. I had just witnessed creation. I had just participated in creation. It was a holy experience and it overwhelmed me.

I remember holding my daughter and weeping uncontrollably. In my heart, I was pledging to love her, to protect her, to care for her. I was undone by the burden, responsibility, and magnitude of it all as I held what had been entrusted to me. I was wearing all the joy and the overwhelming, heartbreaking, sacred beauty of the birthing experience. I was as full of emotion as I had been at any moment in my life, and it showed on my face.

I stood in amazement at what David surely meant when he said, "I am certain that I will see the LORD's goodness in the land of the living" (Ps. 27:13 HCSB). I couldn't know all that would unfold in the life of that little girl. I couldn't know what I would feel to see her walk and talk for the first time. I could have never known what would stir in me when she said my name for the first time, what I would feel when I gave the last running push and took my hand off the back of her bicycle and watched her pedal away independently, or how my heart would break in kissing her small cheek and watching her muster the courage to walk into an unknown kindergarten classroom for the first time.

There was no way of knowing on that day of celebrating her birth in the hallway with friends and family, that months later we'd be in Vanderbilt Children's hospital with her tiny body connected to monitors and tubes, monitoring her little heartbeat, lying next to her, praying, begging God, and thinking I couldn't breathe or live if something happened to this person I had known for only a matter of weeks.

Like the parents I question in class, I had no idea what I had surrendered myself to. I had never really considered why I signed on for this and what I had agreed to. I had absolutely no idea what it would require of me, how it would transform me, and how disruptive the process would be. Dan Allender, PhD, author of *How Children Raise Parents*, spoke well to this:

> There is no relationship on earth in which we are called to be more noble and to sacrifice more deeply than with our children. . . .

No other arena in life holds us more hostage to hope, more afraid to dream, more defensive about our decisions, and more open to receive help—all simultaneously. The intensity and passion of parenting bring the potential not only for our worst, but also for our very best as human beings.[1]

I've seen evidence of good in me that I didn't know existed. I've never been more willing to sacrifice or capable of things I didn't know were humanly possible—staying awake for three consecutive days, giving repeated injections to my own children, or even just waking at 2:00 a.m., out of a dead sleep, and cleaning up vomit! I can still remember waking in the middle of the night with that same sweet girl I held in the hospital room. She woke with the stomach virus and had thrown up all over her little bed, in her long hair, and soaked her pj's. I remember drawing a warm bath and washing that night's regurgitated dinner out of her damp hair while my wife changed the sheets on her bed, only to repeat the whole process three more times before 5:00 a.m. (You know you really love someone when you clean up her vomit repeatedly throughout the night.)

Just as I've never been more willing to sacrifice, I've never felt more selfish. I have tapped into darker parts of me than I knew existed. I'm talking thoughts that shook me to the core. In describing her own journey in parenting, Anne Lamott once said, "I thought such awful thoughts that I cannot even say them out loud because they would make Jesus want to drink gin straight out of the cat dish."[2] Mine were worse; I promise you. I've never felt more angry, entitled, hateful, spiteful, and ashamed than I have as a parent. Parenting really does ignite our capacity for the worst and the best, for good and for harm.

Identify three different moments when you felt helpless as a parent.

What did you take away from those experiences?

What may God have wanted to show you in those moments?

How has parenting changed you as a person?

Become a Student

So where do we go with all this? If we are willing to consider that God designed parenting more for our own sanctification and transformation than to shape our children's lives, we open ourselves up to movement, growth, and maturity. If we consider that God designed parenting as a place where men and women could come to ask hard questions, engage deep heartache, and find renewed hope—a place where people can grow in the range and richness of new possibility in their lives—then there is much room for maturity of heart.

Become a student of your own maturity (or lack thereof). One of the more courageous things we can do as parents is to first identify three individuals in our lives who *know* us. Not people we have surface relationships with, but with whom we share history. These should be people who have seen some of the best and worst of who we are as people—our parents, our spouses, other family members, good friends, trusted coworkers—individuals who aren't afraid to tell us the truth about ourselves. Ask three individuals who fit the above criteria to answer some questions about you, and invite them to give you some honest feedback.

What have you observed about me as a parent?

What are the strengths I bring to parenting?

What are the struggles I bring to parenting?

What do you enjoy about being in relationship with me?

What are the challenges about being in relationship with me?

We all need feedback. We are all incapable of seeing how other people experience us. We live in our own skin; therefore we don't understand what it's like to be in relationship with ourselves. That's why we need input and perspective.

We often invite individuals we work with at Daystar to take a personality inventory called the Enneagram. After answering a series of questions, individuals are assigned a number (1–9) that identifies a profile or personality. It's a fascinating study that reveals strengths and challenges that come with each number. For example, I'm a One on the Enneagram. For those unfamiliar with this inventory, a One is akin to the "type A" personality. I'm driven, focused, task-oriented. As a parent, when I'm at my best as a One, I bring leadership and mission to our family. When I'm at my worst, I plow over the other members of my family, I don't consider them, and I get more focused on my agenda than on people. I need to live with some kind of awareness that both exist in me—the strengths and the challenges. The less aware

I am of both, the more likely I am to operate more (or only) out of one side.

One of the services we offer at Daystar is what we call a *parent consult*. It's different from an assessment, where a family would come in with their child and we'd spend time with all the members of a family. In a consultation, parents come alone and we spend that time discussing some of the current challenges of parenting, questions about what's normal and what isn't, developmental concerns, and so on. I enjoy coming together with parents who are hungry for information in that time, wanting to really understand and study their children. These are parents with intention.

It's not uncommon that these conversations stir a lot of emotions. That's often what happens when we talk about the kids we love. Sometimes parents cry; sometimes they argue; often (most often) they expose something about themselves. Years ago, I met with a set of highly successful parents who had three very young children. They were dealing with a number of the normal challenges that come with parenting in that season of life. There was a range of issues, spanning from sleep behaviors, to academic concerns and one particular fear of the father that his son was no longer interested in doing *any* activities with him. He invited his son to do anything from running errands to shooting hoops in the backyard, and the answer had consistently been some version of no. As he was voicing this concern, it became obvious that he was more angry than sad about his son's stiff-armed approach to relationship with him.

I paused him at one point in the conversation and asked his wife what she had observed about the boy's relationship with his dad. She was beginning to share some thoughts, but kept pausing, seeming to choose her words carefully. At one point, she hesitated and looked up at the ceiling in search of the correct response. Her husband began snapping his fingers in a circular motion, the way a coach does when he wants an athlete to move faster.

I was, at first, confused by his gesture, but then I began to understand his response as she anxiously moved to the edge of her seat and began trying to answer the question more quickly. She looked tense and fearful (the way a third grader looks on a timed math test). I halted the exchange to ask about his response and what the snapping meant within the context of our conversation. He barked, "It *means* hurry up. It means 'Answer the question in a timely fashion' because this consultation is costing me, and I don't want it to be wasted time."

This father may well be a One on the Enneagram, like me. So I took a bit of pity on him (for a brief moment) because we could be cut from the same cloth. I did, however, also see it as an important opportunity to give him some honest feedback. I pushed back with, "I think I'm beginning to understand some of why your son may not be interested in shooting hoops with you in the backyard. Watching you with your wife makes me wonder how many people in your family feel like being in relationship with you is like *work*—like working under a boss who has really high expectations."

Rather than responding with any awareness, curiosity, or humility, he pushed right back with, "Well, I *do* have high expectations, and I'm not going to apologize for that. There's nothing wrong with that."

I enjoy this kind of moment with another father. Not just because I'm a passionate advocate for children and helping

parents understand them better, but because one of the things I
know about my gender is that we can be clueless when it comes
to the art of relationship, and I like seeing the light switch come
on. I get it; I'm a male.

I pushed right back on this powerful dad and said, "It's fine
for you to have expectations of the people around you. What's
not OK is for you to deal with your wife and children like they
are employees who are in line for a performance evaluation.
You are seated next to your life partner, not your secretary. You
are snapping your fingers at her like she's on your payroll. It's
demeaning and disrespectful."

I'm not usually so blunt in my approach to counseling, but
if there's one thing I've learned over the years of working with
boys and men, it's that they need you to be concrete and com-
manding, direct and instructive. They can get lost in too many
metaphors and questions. It's not to say we're stupid (well, some
us are); we're just more linear in our thinking, more singularly
focused, straight shooters. We also have a hard time admitting
we are wrong and tend to blame other people more than owning
our own stuff.

So I tried to communicate with this father as clearly as I
could. I went on to say, "I think you want desperately to connect
with your son. You wouldn't be sitting here if you didn't want
a relationship with him. I'm guessing every time he stiff-arms
you, you feel rejected and it grieves you. It would grieve any dad
who really loves his son. But you've got to pay less attention to
his saying no to you and more attention to yourself. You need
to ask yourself, 'What is going on in me that would potentially
make this boy not want to be in my company when other eight-
year-old boys want desperately to be with their dads?'"

By this point in the conversation, his wife looked like a mix of wanting to cry and wanting to hug me (or bring me a batch of homemade cookies). I went on to challenge this man to consider the possibility that his son likely experienced him more as a corrective coach than an invested father. Being an intentional parent means I study my intention, my purpose in parenting. For this father, his intention was more about instruction, correction, direction, and expectation. He had lost the emphasis of enjoyment, connection, and relationship.

I invited him to find three individuals to ask some of the above questions to, and then to go a step beyond that. I challenged him to sit down with his son, in a posture of humility and curiosity, and to say something like, "I want to be the best dad I can for you. That means I'm going to make some big mistakes along the way. Sometimes I love you so much that I get stuck on teaching you, instructing you, and correcting you. And I don't want to forget to just enjoy you and spend time with you. I want to spend more time with you, and I want to ask you to help me. Would you help me know when I'm doing things and saying things that make you feel really loved? And would you consider forgiving me for getting stuck and give me a chance to practice doing a better job?" I told him to pause there and let his son respond however he wanted to respond, and to resist any urge to justify his position, get teachy, or start lecturing. I think I may have said something to the dad like, "Just stick to the script!"

I then encouraged him to ask the son if he would pick something he'd really love to do on Saturday morning, just the two of them. I told him to tell the boy the only requirement was that it had to be fun for the boy and it had to involve donuts. I reminded this father that it may take time before his son was open to shooting hoops again, but I believed they could eventually get there. "When you do talk him into playing again, I want you to retrieve the ball. Pass it back to him, enjoy him, praise him. Laugh with him, be playful with him, but do not correct his layup, work on his free throw, or critique his dribbling. You are rebuilding right now, and the priority is not instruction or teaching. He has a basketball coach and he just needs you to be his father."

The dad was taking notes, because Ones like a very clear plan and a script. Before he stopped writing, I said, "And if you ever snap your fingers in a circle again, you better be singing with a barbershop quartet, not dealing with a member of your family." We both smiled.

My challenge to that father is a challenge I've extended to myself. I have, in different seasons, asked my own children to give me some feedback on how they experience me as a father. I'm always nervous asking for that feedback. I never know what will come from the mouths of my children. I just know that it scares me to ask, but I want to know. Consider asking your kids questions like . . .

What are some things you enjoy that we do together?

What are some things you wish I would do more of as a dad/ mom?

What are some things you wish I wouldn't do or would do different as a dad/mom?

One of my sons once answered, "I wish you wouldn't iron clothes when we watch a movie." His response was so innocent and so profound. The One in me is a multitasker. I approach watching a movie as a time when I can also iron my dress shirts, fold laundry, or return e-mails. Something about multitasking with those basic chores communicates a message of, "You aren't high-enough priority for me to drop what I'm doing and just enjoy being with you." I get it. I can *so* see where he would arrive at that conclusion. I really do. It just crushed me to hear him say that, and I'm so grateful he felt courageous enough to do so.

Being a student of our children really starts with being a student of us—taking inventory of who we are, knowing the strengths and struggles we bring to parenting, and understanding how our kids experience us.

From there, I think we can begin to better study our children and their *temperament* and *development*. We believe strongly in the study of *development* and *temperament*. There are the unique ways that God designed these extraordinary little beings. Psalm 139 reminds that He knew our "inmost being" from the very start, when we were formed and made in "the secret place" (vv. 13, 15 NIV).

Parenting is a lifelong journey of discovering that brilliant, one-of-a-kind, intentional, creative process of God imprinting on them in the secret place. He permanently wrote on their little hearts before we first laid eyes or hands on them—whether they have light or dark skin; blond, brunette, black, or red hair; whether they bend more toward introversion or extroversion; whether they'll fall in love with medicine, art, teaching, or accounting; and whether they'll be more courageous or more cautious. Many of these traits and so much more make up what we call *temperament*. We want to engage a long, slow journey of studying temperament—the unique hard wiring that is imprinted onto the design of our children. We must parent in tandem with that design, not in opposition to it.

It's not uncommon for the three of us to come together with a parent in our offices who says something like, "I understand his oldest brother. We share so many of the same interests and passions. His younger sister is almost identical to her mother in about every way, but our middle son is a mystery to us." Whether he is a mystery or more familiar, our job is to become a student—to seek to understand the work that God began and is faithfully completing in the lives of our children. Our job is to steward that, not change it.

In addition to temperament, we want to study *development*. Development is the understanding of why certain events take place at specific times in the lives of our children. There are reasons why you don't start kindergarten at three or drive a car at ten. We don't have the skills—the physical, cognitive, and emotional skills—to attempt certain tasks. We've identified developmental milestones that serve as markers for what we expect to see children accomplish at specific moments in their lives. When we don't see evidence of meeting developmental milestones on time, it invites us to look a bit closer and consider offering some additional support to further the developmental process.

When we teach classes across the country on understanding boys and girls, we talk about how girls and boys move at different paces in their development and of the importance of understanding the role that gender plays in development.

It is so encouraging to be with a group of parents and to speak about some of the developmental norms and see parents sigh in relief while discovering that experimenting with lying is normal at a certain age, or that there's a reason why toddler boys rarely sit still but are constantly in motion. When we understand a child's temperament and development, it serves as a backdrop to our discipline, instruction, and relationship. We diminish the chance of getting roadblocked, stuck, or frustrated when we discover that an introverted child will likely melt down Sunday afternoon if he or she goes to school all week long, attends a high school football game on Friday night, attends a sibling's soccer game on Saturday morning, goes to a birthday party Saturday afternoon and to church on Sunday, and then has family friends over for lunch after church. That child simply needs moments when he/she can retreat and refuel. Too much relationship and activity over-stimulates and burdens your introverted child.

How would you define your child's temperament from being a student of your child?

What are some specific ways you can creatively work within your child's temperament rather than against it?

Speak a Better Story

We've asked you to consider that being an intentional parent involves a good amount of reflection and perspective, and study and understanding. Now we'll add to that list of ingredients vision and investment. Donald Miller, in his book *A Million Miles in a Thousand Years*, remarked:

> We spend years actually living . . . stories, and expect our lives to feel meaningful. The truth is, if what we choose to do

with our lives won't make a story meaningful, it won't make a life meaningful either. . . .

We live in a world where bad stories are told, stories that teach us life doesn't mean anything and that humanity has no great purpose. It's a good calling, then, to speak a better story.[3]

I started thinking more about Miller's words and began wondering about the story my life was telling. Research tells us that children learn more from watching adults than from being told how to behave and feel. I began thinking about what I was modeling. I began wondering how my kids would describe me to people who didn't know me. I began wondering about the stories my own sons would tell their sons one day about what kind of father I was. Actually, I became worried and concerned about what they'd say, how they'd describe me, and the stories they'd tell.

I can remember driving down the interstate in a red convertible with the top down on my honeymoon. My new bride and I were having this thoughtful conversation about our new life together, talking about places across the globe we wanted to see, things we wanted to do, who we wanted to be. It was the kind of hope-filled, dream-saturated, non-reality-based conversation you have when you are in your early twenties, newly married, and clueless about all that will unfold in the years to come.

We've been to a handful of those places, tried a few of those adventures we committed to, but I'm not sure how much we resemble who we wanted to be. I do know we both wanted to be parents, and God chose to honor that particular desire.

I remember being in the hospital after my daughter's birth, when all the friends and family had gone home, and we were alone for the first time with this new life. We had a similar conversation about things we wanted to do with our children, who we wanted to be as parents, and how we wanted our family to operate. We've hit some of those marks and missed some.

Vision Casting

What did come out of those conversations was a vision for our family. What came next were some deliberate decisions about living out that vision. This requires us being proactive more than being reactive. A good way to jump-start this process is by *writing a family mission statement*. Put into words what you want to be about as a family, define your core values, and develop some family goals from that place.

Another tool for casting a vision is *a time/activity assessment*. Make a list of all the things you do as a family during a given week—sleep, eat, commute to school and work, watch TV, check e-mail, read updates on Facebook, text, play sports, create or listen to music, take art lessons, participate in extracurricular activities, enjoy friends, attend church, shop, volunteer, surf the Net, or talk on the phone. The list should include the activities that define the daily life of each member of the family. Go back through the list and assign a weekly or monthly amount of time spent engaged in the activity. Approximate the number of hours spent in each activity.

On a separate sheet of paper, make a list of the necessary things in life (sleep, eat, work/school, etc.). After that, add those activities that didn't make the first list but that you'd like to have as a part of the life of your family—visiting or calling extended family members, outreach, playing board games, hospitality, reading time, and so on.

You may be surprised by what makes the list, what doesn't make the list, or the amount of time you spend engaged in different activities. Next, compare both lists to the family mission statement. See where the activities align with the core values and mission. Identify where the present activities line up with the family goals. This kind of time/activity assessment can be a valuable tool for living a better story.

Consider replacing a spring break, Christmas, or summer vacation tradition with a trip of a different kind—a local or overseas mission trip, a staycation that is less focused on travel and more focused on time together; a long-standing tradition becomes an adventure-based experience. Be creative with this.

What kind of story are you living in front of your children?

Does your life speak about the things you believe and the people you love?

Are you living a life of faith in front of your children, or just talking about it?

Psalm 127:3–5 says,

> Sons are a heritage from the LORD,
>   children a reward from him.
> Like arrows in the hands of a warrior
>   are sons born in one's youth.
> Blessed is the man
>   whose quiver is full of them.
> They will not be put to shame
>   when they contend with their enemies in the gate.
>   (NIV)

That image of an arrow in the hand of a warrior is powerful. An arrow in the hand of a warrior has the power of protection and provision. You don't release an arrow recklessly into the air. To do so could bring about great harm and destruction. And yet, there's plenty of evidence of that in the world today. We see children released recklessly every day without the intention and precision with which a warrior releases an arrow.

That's what our children need from us. They need us to step into this great responsibility with precision and intention. They need us to be aware of ourselves and aware of them. They need us to study the process and to understand and handle them with care. They need us to be thoughtful with our words and our decisions.

Most important, they need us to lean into the One who made these unique gifts we've been entrusted with. They need us to remember they were made in a secret place with great precision and intention, and to handle their gifts accordingly.

2.

Being a Patient Parent

—with Sissy

MY FAMILY WAS NOT ATHLETIC. WE WEREN'T THE type to go on bike rides or hikes together growing up. We didn't play family rounds of golf or tennis. We didn't center our vacations around an activity, other than a few snow skiing trips on which I consistently came down with altitude sickness. We just weren't—and aren't—super athletic. But we loved to fish.

When I was a little girl, my dad would take me to the nearest river or lake and we'd sit for hours fishing for bass or crappie. As I got older, the fishing became more intense. It moved from fresh water to salt water. My dad's company bought a sportfishing boat, and I learned the art of deep-sea fishing. By the time my sister (who is sixteen years younger than I am) was growing up, our family vacations centered around an activity . . . fishing. She is a natural. She throws a hook in any type of water and comes up with some type of fish.

Now, you may not know much about deep-sea fishing. I sure didn't until we had our own boat, called the *Inn Heaven* (our dad was in the Holiday Inn business . . . get it?). In Deep-Sea Fishing 101, *Inn Heaven*–style, we learned that there were two types of deep-sea fishing: bottom fishing and trolling.

Bottom fishing is what most boats you rent in the tropics do. They take you out and drop an anchor somewhere off a coral reef. You fish for grouper and yellowtail snapper, and periodically catch a grunt or a queen triggerfish. Things move a lot more quickly bottom fishing. Patience is required, as with all types of fishing, but it's more of a short-term type of patience with speedier results. There are days when we'd only catch a few fish, and days when every time we'd drop our bait, we'd catch something.

Trolling is completely different. When you're trolling, you let out those big poles you see on top of sportfishing boats. They have eight or so lines out at a time, mostly with artificial lures. You try to catch really big fish when you're trolling, such as wahoo, tuna, or dolphin (not the cute dolphin mammals, but dolphinfish—the ones with flat, angry faces that are called mahimahi on your plate). The trophy fish of the trolling community is a marlin; they are blue, black, or white, depending on the part of the world in which you are fishing. They're often the silver-and-blue fish with a sail-type fin and a long, pointy nose that you see hanging in restaurants in Florida. When trolling, you can fish for days and never get a bite. It takes more of the long-suffering type of patience to troll. (And let me just say, if you are a professional fisherman reading this, I'm sure you are getting a good laugh. Don't forget, this is Deep-Sea Fishing 101 on the *Inn Heaven*, as told by Sissy, not by Captain Ahab.)

So, what in the world does deep-sea fishing have to do with being a patient parent, you may be asking? A lot. Because fishing and parenting are two of the most patience-requiring activities in the world. Plus, there are days they both can make you want to throw up over the side of the boat. Parenting and fishing both require two predominant types of patience.

Bottom-Fishing Patience

I can clearly remember when my sister was in her toddler years: *everything* she did was slow. She ate slowly; she walked slowly; she asked questions slowly; she even ran slowly. It took her at least ten minutes to get out of the car *every time.* I remember vividly pulling up to our house after running errands one day, when Kathleen said to me, "Thithy [the toddler version of *Sissy* when you have a lisp], why are you always in such a hurry?" Her question hit me like a ton of bricks. She was right. I was constantly trying to hurry her. I had no patience to wait. I still don't have much, twenty years later. But what I do have now is Google. And because I don't naturally know what patience looks like, I Googled it.

WikiHow gave some wonderful ideas on "How to Be Patient."[1] It gave wise instruction such as, "Always remember that you will eventually get what you want." Really? I'm not sure about your world, but this isn't true in mine . . . especially when I'm in a hurry! "Always have a positive outlook in life." Tell me that again when my son has just failed the seventh grade. And, lastly, and maybe most crushingly, "People who are patient tend to have better lives." Great. Just great. So, how in the world do I get there when patience doesn't come naturally for me? And I'm guessing it might not come naturally for you, either, since you are reading this chapter.

Let's start with bottom fishing. A few examples of the bottom fishing patience scenarios might be:

- Your three-year-old daughter draws on your dining room wall with a crayon.
- Your seven-year-old son loses the Nook he just got for his birthday.
- Your twelve-year-old daughter rolls her eyes at you . . . again.
- Your fifteen-year-old son gets Saturday school for being disrespectful to a teacher.

What would you add to this list from your own parenting?

When was the last time you lost your temper, and why?

Bottom-fishing patience comes in to play in the daily dealings with your child—those little, irritating issues that come up and try your patience. In chapter 5, "Being a Consistent Parent," we'll talk about ideas for discipline in these scenarios and many more. But for now, let's talk about what to do with *you*. Or what you can do with you when you start to lose your patience.

A few simple bottom-fishing suggestions:

BREATHE. It sounds awfully simple. And it is. Slow yourself and your responses down just a little. Count to ten. Take deep breaths, as if you're trying to get over the nausea caused by deep-sea fishing (or the situation that just came up). Breathing gets more oxygen to your brain, slows down your nervous system, and gives you time to think. Ask yourself if you're frustrated with your child or frustrated in general, because one can easily bleed over into the other.

LISTEN. Be present. Much of our frustration often comes from the fact that we're doing too many things at once. You're hurrying out the door. Your son is trying to tie his shoes. Your daughter drops her backpack while she's telling you about a fight she had with her brother. Slow down. Stop and listen to what she's saying. A child who rambles in conversation is sometimes only waiting for you to give her your full attention. Being present can help you focus on her and forget the other distractions that are nagging at you and your patience.

GIVE HIM A CHANCE. Sometimes we get angry with children for doing the wrong thing before we've even given them time to do the right thing. Remember, all children move slowly at times, just like my sister did. "Hurry," or the need for it, doesn't compute in their brains like it does in ours. You may need to give a time frame. For example, dinner is over at 7:00 p.m. Give a child who eats slowly a time limit—one that might last a little longer than yours. This can help ease the pressure he feels to perform, while at the same time teaching him a little more of the science of hurrying. It can also give you a parameter around the endless "one more bites" that so often turn a good meal miserable.

GIVE HER THE BENEFIT OF THE DOUBT. Your nine-year-old daughter made a huge mess of the kitchen. You come downstairs and immediately lose your temper over the milk, cracked eggs, and butter all over your counter. Breathe. Give her the benefit of the doubt. What was she trying to do? Was she purposely making a mess? Or was she making you a surprise breakfast? The difference in her motives can do quite a bit to dictate the difference in your response.

KEEP A SENSE OF HUMOR. While pigtails on your new puppy may be frustrating to you, it's awfully funny to a four-year-old. Your humor and your child's are quite different. Your son or daughter may not have intended to be bad. Just funny. He may not even have known that it was wrong. He needs your wisdom more than your frustration in those moments. And in safe and harmless situations, a little laughter can go a long way in helping you connect.

THINK ABOUT YOUR CHILD'S CAPABILITIES. How old is she? What is she really able to do? Are you frustrated with your child's lack of time awareness when he can't even tell time yet? Think of ways to make things relatable to him. For example, use your child's favorite television show as a time reference. My sister counted off everything by "How many Bill Cosbys until we have to go?" It's important to be aware of your child's abilities cognitively, developmentally, and physically. He may not be old enough yet to pick up his room or do chores without a lot of reminders from you. If that's the case, draw a chart, which we'll talk more about in the chapter on consistency. Charts are incredibly helpful for young children. And you can make picture charts even before they can read. Study up on child development to understand your child's capabilities and ease your frustration.

ALLOW DOWNTIME IN YOUR CHILD'S SCHEDULE. Don't keep your days so packed that you can't keep up. When you live rushing from activity to activity, you don't give yourself time to stop and enjoy life or your child. It can keep you revved up to a pace where it's much easier to get frustrated.

GIVE YOURSELF A TIME-OUT. If you notice that you are really frustrated, you may need to do more than breathe. You may need to walk away from the situation. A very appropriate and parental response is, "We'll talk about this in a few minutes." It gives kids time to think about what they've done and offers you a much-needed moment to regulate your frustration. Honestly, yelling never helps. It just creates more strife between you and your child and either angers him or makes him fearful. Again, we'll come back to more appropriate responses in the chapter on consistency. But for now, don't be afraid to take a time-out. You will be doing yourself and your child a favor.

START FIFTEEN MINUTES EARLY. How many times do you lose your patience just because you're running late? If you consistently started fifteen minutes early, from the very beginning of your day, we would guess that you would get back more than 15 percent of the peace in your household. Set your watch and clocks ahead if it helps. Your patience and relationship with your child are worth much more than the extra fifteen minutes of sleep . . . or time on the computer . . . or whatever is competing for your time.

KNOW YOUR PATIENCE WILL BE CHALLENGED. Every child is difficult at times. Part of being a parent is raising a child to be his or her own person. And, being his own person means that he will have to test the strength of his will. Children most often test their wills against their parents, and that testing often comes at the expense of your patience. Know that they will push you and your limits. They'll challenge your authority.

They'll test your boundaries on the road to becoming who God has made them to be.

Proverbs 17:21 in *The Message* says, "Having a fool for a child is misery; it's no fun being the parent of a dolt." Every child will act like a fool, at least once in their lives, whether it's by pouring Cheerios on their heads or failing a spelling test. They will. And when they do, they will try your patience. But Proverbs 17 also says, in verse 14, "The start of a quarrel is like a leak in a dam, so stop it before it bursts" (MSG). Remember these ten points to being a more patient parent in the short-term. They can help you keep your cool and stop the leak before the dam bursts and sends you over into the realm of trolling.

Trolling Patience

You may have read this last section and thought something like, *I wish my child would pour Cheerios on his head. We're way past that. I'm so tired of having to pick him up from a party or a friend's house drunk. Or, I don't know what I'll do if one more parent calls and says my daughter has been mean to hers. I've heard about mean girls all my life. I can't believe my daughter would turn out to be one. I'm so tired of it.*

One dad I talked to the other day said, "Can we just get around this whole narcissistic thing?" His daughter was seventeen and giving him fits with her disrespect. She rolled her eyes, threw out "Whatever's," and gave him one- or two-word sentences constantly. My wise and experienced response was, "She's in her narcissistic years. It's a phase, even though it's a miserable one. Keep trying."

"Every time I try, she rejects me," he said.

"I know, but she still needs to know that you want to spend time with her."

"Okay, I know I'm harping on this, but this narcissistic phase is just causing us a *lot* of problems."

It may be that you're exhausted by your adolescent's narcissistic phase and how *everything* is about her *all* of the time. (I sound a little bit like her, don't I?) Or it may be that it has been weeks since you've had a civil conversation with your son. Or that your daughter hasn't cared about school for months and is bringing home all Ds and Fs.

Whatever the challenge, if it's moved over into the trolling realm, it's trying your patience long term. It's wearying. You're exhausted. Your kids are discouraged or angry, or both. And you feel, on some days, like giving up.

When do you get the most discouraged as a parent?

How do you see your discouragement affecting your child?

Romans 5:3 and 2 Peter 1:6 use the phrase "passionate patience" (MSG). That is the phrase trolling brings to my mind, whether it comes to parenting or fishing.

About ten years ago, my dad sold his sportfishing boat. My sister and I were devastated. So he made a deal with us that every time we take a family vacation now somewhere near an ocean, we get to spend a day fishing.

Several years ago, we went to Hawaii and went trolling with Captain Michael. For some reason, Captain Michael didn't believe we were very experienced fishers. He didn't really want to let my dad help him untie the boat. His explanation of how to hold the poles was a little too lengthy. And he let me have it when I was trying to bring in a fish.

If you've ever been trolling before, you know how exciting it is when the line all of a sudden starts to make the whirring sound that means the fish has taken the bait. Someone yells from the deck to the captain to "Stop the boat!" He runs down the ladder, yelling at everyone to pull the rest of the lines in. He puts someone in the chair to have the lucky job of bringing in the fish, and the fun begins. Or, at least it's supposed to. On this day, it was more than fun that began for me. It was something closer to panic.

"You're not holding your rod right!" So I held it a little higher.

"You're not moving the line back and forth in the reel. You have to do that!!" I'm not sure I ever said a word.

"Hold the rod higher."

"Bring it in faster! Faster! Faster!!"

I was starting to perspire. I reeled as fast and as high as I could for twenty-five minutes with him yelling constantly. Finally, there was another loud noise on the line. "Well, you lost it!" was all the captain discouragingly said (or yelled), and he climbed back up the ladder.

Trying to be a patient parent can feel like fishing with Captain Michael. You work and work and work, and then, in the midst of a lot of yelling, things fall apart. Everything on Captain Michael's boat was communicated with a great deal of emotion, as it probably is, on some days, in your home. Parenting, in general, calls forth heaps of passion. Dictionary.com's first definition of *passion* is "any powerful or compelling emotion or feeling, as love or hate."[2] Your children feel strong, powerful emotions. You are often compelled to respond with equally powerful emotions. We would say that kind of emotion flying around your home (or boat) requires passionate patience.

> So don't lose a minute in building on what you've been given, complementing your basic faith with good character, spiritual understanding, alert discipline, *passionate patience*, reverent wonder, warm friendliness, and generous love, each dimension fitting into and developing the others. With these qualities active and growing in your lives, no grass will grow under your feet, no day will pass without its reward as you mature in your experience of our Master Jesus. Without these qualities you can't see what's right before you. (2 Peter 1:5–9 MSG, emphasis added)

Seeing what's right before you is often what requires the most patience. Well, let's get this correct: you see part of what's right before you. You see the temper tantrums, the disrespect, the entitlement . . . and that becomes all you see. You see your child's *behavior*, but not your *child* in those moments. And so you react. You match his or her intensity of emotion, but with frustration rather than passionate patience. So, how do you get there in those trolling types of situations? We have a few suggestions that we hope are much gentler than Captain Michael's.

TAKE CARE OF YOURSELF. When I was in supervision to get my license as a counselor, if there was one thing my supervisor stressed, it was self-care. She said repeatedly that for me to offer consistent care for others, I had to be caring for myself. As a counselor, that meant having outlets, making sure I was attending to my own issues, and so on. As a parent, it looks a little different, but not much. Self-care, for you, exists on both a practical and a deeper level. Practically, get good sleep. Eat well—healthy, of course, but also cook things *you* love, not just your child's favorite meals. Learn to relax. Take a yoga class. Paint. Go for walks. Have a date night with your spouse. Go on a guys' or girls' trip. TiVo your favorite shows, not just cartoons. Watch a movie. Take a bath. Doing the things you love gives you space and time to enjoy being yourself, which frees you up to enjoy your children being themselves.

DON'T TAKE THINGS TOO PERSONALLY. I remember, a few years ago, a mom who lost her patience with her children often. In a joint mother/daughter counseling session, it came out that she really believed her children left their shoes in the den on purpose. She believed that it meant they didn't think she was a good enough mother to pick up their things in her home. It felt like that to her. It may feel like that to you—every once in a while, or a lot. It was personal for this tired mom. But it wasn't for her children. They weren't thinking about her when they left their shoes out. The children were thinking about their hurting feet, or sliding down the hall in their socks, or some other fun idea. The teenagers were thinking about themselves, which is most of what they think about anyway—the narcissistic years, remember?

ASSUME THE BEST. In nineteen years of counseling children, teens, and families, I believe this is one of the most importance concepts to learn as a family. Assume the best of each other. It's also one of the hardest to master. Your children are not out to get you. They're usually not trying to hurt you, although they may be sometimes. They love you and respect you, even when they don't act like it. Just as in the case of the little girl who made a mess making breakfast for her mom and dad, many kids make mistakes when they genuinely are trying their best. He may be struggling with school because of a learning challenge. She may be unresponsive because she's depressed. There is often a bigger picture going on than your child's reaction to you, or lack of one. Assume the best, and ask questions to find out the truth of what's happening. Many teens, especially, talk to me about feeling accused by their parents. Ask questions. And if you suspect that they're not telling the truth, be a good detective to find out. Assuming the best will help you and your child feel more positively toward each other in particular and life in general.

BE AWARE OF YOUR EXPECTATIONS. We talked before about being aware of what your child is capable of. This continues to matter in the long term. Does your daughter keep getting in trouble with her friends because she doesn't know how to say no? Are you pressuring your son to make As when he really is a B or C student? Are you expecting your child to be kind and gracious to adults all of the time? Are you expecting your son to naturally write thank-you notes without being reminded, or your shy daughter to be the president of her student body? What are you expecting from your child? Are your expectations in line with who he or she is? Sometimes children can be taught to rise to your expectations, and sometimes their God-given strengths may simply be in other areas.

BE PREPARED FOR FAILURE. Your child will fail. In Melissa's and my book *Modern Parents, Vintage Values*, we talk about Romans 5:3–4. It says, "suffering produces perseverance; perseverance, character; and character, hope" (NIV). It goes on to say that "hope does not disappoint us." In the book, we then say, "Your children will."[3] They will disappoint you. They will fail. They are sinners, just like you and me. And honestly, you'd rather them fail at home. At home, you have a chance to support and give them consequences, but won't when they're no longer living under your roof.

GIVE THEM TOOLS TO DEAL WITH THEIR EMOTIONS. Believe it or not, you have the tools at this stage of life to manage your emotions. You can learn patience, both bottom-fishing and trolling types. But self-control genuinely is much harder for them. The frontal lobe of the brain—the portion of the brain that helps understand consequences, sees the difference between positive and negative actions,[4] and manages emotions[5]—is not finished developing until the early twenties. Therefore, your child sometimes truly doesn't know how to regulate himself emotionally. He needs your help. Teach her to express herself emotionally, but respectfully. Kids are not going to naturally know how to join the two. "I think that's so stupid," could instead be, "Dad, that makes me really frustrated. Can you tell me why we can't get a new puppy when we just brought my little sister home from the hospital?" We like to use the phrase, "Try again." You don't necessarily have to discipline every time they speak disrespectfully. But you can help remind them to try again till they communicate clearly and with respect. Give them outlets for their emotions as well. In parenting seminars, David advocates a punching bag or Bozo Bop bag for boys to let out their aggression. I teach many girls to write in journals or to draw what they're feeling. A Bozo Bop can be good for girls from time to time too. Children and teens don't know what to do with their feelings. We can help. And as we help them manage their emotions, it can help us to manage ours as well.

REMEMBER YOUR CHILDHOOD. Kids say often to me, "My parents think I have it so easy. They tell me I don't have anything to worry about other than school. But I do. I have so much. I go to school for eight hours every day; then I have homework. I have to worry about friends and family and boys/girls. It's a lot more than they remember." It is important for you to remember, and it's so easy to forget. It's easy for us to think things like, *They don't know what real problems are,* or *I wish the biggest thing I worried about was who to play with at recess,* but who to play with at recess or sit with at lunch can be the most anxiety-producing portion of your child's day. I see kids who literally have panic attacks during those periods. It is hard to be a kid, and even harder to be a teenager. Take some time to journal what life was like at your child's age. What did you think about? What did you worry about the most? Who was important to you? What were you afraid of? If it's hard for you to remember, talk to a parent or a sibling or a childhood friend. And if you had a hard childhood, it doesn't mean that your child's experience is easier. I tell kids often that if the most painful thing you've ever done is stub your toe, stubbing your toe hurts badly. The emotions and stress your child feels are important and valid, no matter what is causing them. Listen. Remember what it was like for you. Your memories can help you understand and have more compassion for what life is like for them.

LEARN YOUR TRIGGERS. As a parent, you will notice that certain children try your patience more than others. Specific situations cause you to become angry more quickly or cause you to react in a way that surprises you. What are your triggers? What or who causes you to lose your patience? A very important truth about triggers is that they often have more to do with you than with your child. If, for example, your reaction is angrier than the situation warrants, the issue potentially lies more with you than with your child. If you can't recover when your daughter is left out again, or find yourself yelling at the coach or your son when he misses the game-winning soccer goal, it may be about you. Watch your responses. Listen to your reactions. In our DVD curriculum *Raising Boys and Girls*, Melissa speaks beautifully about how your childhood has a profound effect on your parenting. What hurt you then will be touched inside of you when it hurts your child. What made you angry *as* a child can make you angry *at* your child, even though it is not his fault. Learn your triggers, and then deal with them. It's important that you have someone or a group of people who can walk alongside you. You need at least one person who will listen and be honest enough to tell you the truth. At times, it may be important to seek professional counsel. We meet with terrific parents every day who are doing the best they can, but have issues of their own that are stirred up by the issues of their children. It's inevitable. But how different would your life be if your parents had paid attention to and even dealt with their own triggers? Give your children that gift.

WATCH YOUR FUSE. Cindy and Rob are married parents. Rob has a long fuse and Cindy has a short one. The short-fused parent blows up often, but then, five minutes later, forgets the situation and goes back to enjoying her child. Rob simmers. It takes him much longer to lose his patience. But when he does, it takes him equally long to recover. Do you have a long or short fuse? Both types of fuses blow, and that can be equally destructive to a child. Watch your fuse. Learn what sets it off. Hopefully, a few of these ideas can help you stop the fuse before you and your impatience become destructive.

PRAY LIKE CRAZY. Galatians 5 assures us that the fourth fruit of the Spirit is patience. Because it's a fruit of the Spirit, God is the one who produces it in us as we seek Him. Pray that God will develop passionate patience in you.

Which of these suggestions do you struggle with the most?

What could you do practically to give yourself an opportunity for more patience?

What could you do spiritually to experience more of God's passionate patience with you?

Your children will try your patience. They will act like fools. And you will, at times, feel like you're being tossed about on a boat in the high seas, with no fish in sight.

> There's more to come: We continue to shout our praise even when we're hemmed in with troubles, because we know how troubles can develop passionate patience in us, and how that patience in turn forges the tempered steel of virtue, keeping us alert for whatever God will do next. In alert expectancy such as this, we're never left feeling shortchanged. Quite the contrary—we can't round up enough containers to hold everything God generously pours into our lives through the Holy Spirit! (Rom. 5:3–5 MSG)

Today, you may feel like you can't see all that's before you. You can't see past the hurt, or the anger, or the narcissism of your child. But God can change that. Practice these ideas. Pray like crazy that He will produce patience in you as you love your son or daughter. He can and will create a passionate patience in you that will keep you alert for whatever God will do next. And He will not leave you shortchanged. He wants your heart and your family to be overflowing, not with frustration, but with all of the good He longs to give.

3.

Being a Grown-Up Parent

—with Melissa

HE IS. HE NEEDS. SHE IS. SHE NEEDS. THESE statements form the outline for our parenting curriculum, *Raising Boys and Girls*. When we teach on development, David and Sissy go back and forth, talking about the stages in girls and boys' lives—who they are and what they need at each particular stage.

As they talk, I usually watch. I partly watch them because they're a little bit like the Donny and Marie of parenting, minus the sequins and white suits with wide lapels. I watch them and then I watch you, the parents. There are always several parents who are furiously taking notes on their outlines. There are a few high-tech parents typing on their iPads. There are a handful of parents who look like they're typing on their phones, but are really just texting or on Facebook. And then

43

there are the parents who are sitting. Staring. Lost. These parents have moved past the "He is" and "He needs" to "I was" and "I needed." It happens at every parenting seminar we teach.

It may happen in your home too. Your daughter makes a simple comment, and all of a sudden, you're transported back to your own childhood. Rather than hearing *her* words, you hear the words of your mother . . . critical, demanding, and shaming. And your response, in that moment, comes more from the child you were than the parent you are. Rather than speaking like a grown-up, you speak like a ten- or fourteen-year-old. You go back. The situation triggers an emotion in you that takes you back to a certain place in time . . . a time in which you have perhaps gotten stuck.

Being a Stuck Parent

All children pass through stages of development. There are normal developmental milestones we reach on the way to growing up. A baby learns to follow objects with his eyes. A five-year-old learns to dress and undress without help. Puberty begins at an average age of eleven for a girl and thirteen for a boy, and so on.

But sometimes, along the road of normal development, a child can become stuck. If a child is abused verbally or physically, if a child is neglected physically or emotionally, if a child has a significant illness or experiences some type of trauma . . . all of these factors and more can cause a child to stop the normal progression of his or her development. The child's body continues to grow, but his or her emotional maturity stops in that particular area. As a result, a forty-two-year-old father can have parts of his identity that seem more like a fourteen-year-old boy. A seventy-year-old grandmother can have experiences that make her feel and respond like the seven-year-old she was when she suffered physical abuse. Basically, being stuck means that behaviors, beliefs, and emotions connected to unresolved childhood experiences can still be triggered today. And for an adult who is stuck, parenting can be one of the most profoundly triggering experiences of your life.

The following are comments from children we've seen in counseling:

- "My dad doesn't notice me or ever talk to me. But his mom died when he was eleven years old."
- "My mom is not a nurturer. She's embarrassed to say, 'I love you' or hug me. I think her mom was really critical of her. She just hates herself sometimes."
- "My mom and dad never miss a basketball game. They're really into what I do . . . and they make me do a lot. I should be grateful, I know. Sometimes, though, I wish I didn't have to play basketball. I would just like to play in the creek. But I'm all they have. And they didn't have parents who did things for them as much."
- "My dad says I need to cook and prepare the meals" (spoken by a third grader). She looked at me with bewilderment and said, "I don't know how to cook. My dad says he's too tired to do it and he's too old to learn."
- "Sometimes my dad explodes and yells. He's never hit me, but I'm afraid he will. He says it's because I set him off. I do stupid things."

These children who came in for counseling all had one thing in common—their parents were parenting out of their own past needs and hurts. Because of pain, neglect, or abuse, they had all gotten stuck along the way. And their parenting, at times, had more to do with managing their own pain than being the parents their children needed.

Maybe you grew up with a mother who had outbursts of anger. Maybe your father was depressed. Maybe you never found a group of friends who accepted you. As a result, when your child yells at you, you react with emotions that are based more on your past experience than on what's happening in the moment. Maybe your response is stronger than the situation warrants. Maybe you walk away feeling like it's you that wasn't asked to a sleepover, rather than your daughter. Parenting *will* trigger and awaken those unresolved needs and hurts in your life. When that happens, you will see, feel, and reason much like a child.

What are you aware of that feels unresolved from your childhood?

When, in your parenting, do you find yourself acting more like a child or teenager than an adult?

How do you act in those moments?

What is it about those situations in particular that could be touching on something from your past?

"When I was a child, I talked like a child, I thought like a child, I reasoned like a child. When I became a man, I put the ways of childhood behind me" (1 Cor. 13:11 NIV). Putting the ways of childhood behind us can feel insurmountable at times. We all have memories where we were left out, hurt, abandoned, or neglected. It could be that we missed a developmental milestone or never passed through an entire stage of our development. But Paul, in his letter to the Corinthians, still challenges us to put the ways of childhood behind us.

How do we do that? How do we deal with unresolved issues from our growing up? One of the ways we mistakenly deal with it is to compensate. We become what we wish we were, or we offer what we wish we had. Parenting becomes more about what we needed then than what our child needs now. As a result, we develop certain styles of parenting, styles that we subtly believe will protect us and/or our children from the pain that lurks underneath. These five styles are identified as the Peter Pan Parent, the Hovering Parent, the Hipster Parent, the Second-Chance Parent, and the Pain-Free Parent.

The Peter Pan Parent

He is: unwilling to grow up. Peter is the quintessential child. His life is full of fairies, pirates, and thimbles that are really kisses. It is a world of imagination and adventure, and one that was created by a man who was stuck in parts of his own childhood. J. M. Barrie's mother couldn't recover from the death of his brother. So he took to reading to her, entertaining her with his imagination and stories, to help ease her pain. His childhood was colored by the sorrow of his mother. "He struggled all of his life with the pall cast over his childhood self by trauma and loss," wrote D. H. Lawrence.[1] Barrie wrote, "The horror of my boyhood was that I knew a time would come when I also must give up the games, and how it was to be done I saw naught . . . I felt that I must continue playing in secret."[2]

Several books have been written about the grown-up Peter Pans. Rumor has it that there may eventually be a DSM diagnostic code for a personality disorder called the Peter Pan Syndrome, for a person who is unwilling to take responsibility, unable to make commitments to anything or anyone. In short, Peter Pans are unwilling or unable to grow up.

What does this look like in a parent? It looks like the proverbially fun parent. This father or mother is determined to make all things fun. He loves being loved. She enjoys being enjoyed. And if the fun stops, his desperate feelings of inadequacy will surface and he may be left alone.

He needs: courage. Peter was able to fight pirates and befriend wild Indians. But he was terrified of Wendy and anything serious. The Peter Pan Parent can look courageous when he or she takes risks and involves the children in wild adventures. But risk-taking and courage are not synonymous. If you lean toward a Peter Pan style of parenting, your child needs you to have the courage to be an adult parent, rather than just a playmate. Being fun all the time may cause your children to enjoy you, but they will not respect you in the long run. Children find safety in structure. They want you to have boundaries and even discipline them when they misbehave. They need you to talk to them about tough topics like puberty and sex. They feel safe knowing that you are in charge. They will find confidence in your courage. And so will you, as you take the ultimate risk of growing up.

The Hovering Parent

She is: controlled by fear. The hovering parent is trapped by the fear of her own past. She doesn't let her third-grade daughter spend the night out because she doesn't want her to be abused in the way she was. She doesn't let her adolescent son date because she doesn't want him to make the same mistakes with girls that she made with boys in high school. She is a protective parent turned up ten degrees. She hovers in the hopes that she'll protect and prevent her child from facing the same pain she faced . . . *or didn't.*

A hovering parent feels a general sense of anxiety regarding most things involving his or her child. She doesn't necessarily say it out loud, but the fear undergirds her beliefs and actions. As a counselor, I believe that unspoken feelings and fears become more powerful the longer they live inside of us. If you feel disproportionately anxious at times, talk to your spouse, a friend, or a trusted counselor. Talking about it cannot only help uncover what you're afraid of but also cause the fear to lose its pervasive power.

She needs: trust. This parent, more than anything, needs trust. It's not that she should trust that her child has perfect behavior or that no one will ever harm her. But she can trust in a God who protects us, a God who doesn't let anything happen to us that we can't bear, and a God who redeems our deepest hurts.

If you are this parent, remember that God loves your children more than you could ever imagine. He has their good in mind, and even those things that Satan intends for harm, God will turn about for their good. Trust. Trust Him in a way that frees you to parent out of love, rather than fear. And trust Him in a way that invites your child to know and trust in a God who is his Savior and Redeemer.

The Hipster Parent

He is: insecure. The stage of adolescence is a stage Sissy and I call the Narcissistic Years, in *Raising Girls*. In his book *Wild Things*, David calls an adolescent boy the Wanderer. Teenagers are wandering, narcissistic, insecure creatures. In their minds, it's all about them. Many of today's adolescents are preoccupied with looking like "hipsters."

Hipster is a term defined on UrbanDictionary.com as "a sub-culture of men and women typically in their 20's and 30's [based on the Daystar demographic, we would also add teens] that value independent thinking, counter-culture, progressive politics, an appreciation of art and indie-rock, creativity, intelligence, and witty banter." It goes on to say, "Although 'hipsterism' is really a state of mind, it is also often intertwined with distinct fashion sensibilities. Hipsters reject the culturally-ignorant attitudes of mainstream consumers, and are often seen wearing vintage and thrift store inspired fashions, tight-fitting jeans, old-school sneakers, and sometimes thick rimmed glasses. Both hipster men and women sport similar androgynous hair-styles that include combinations of messy shag cuts and asymmetric side-swept bangs."[3]

In Christine Rosen's article "The Hipster Curse: The Parents Who Don't Want to Be Adults," she describes the lives and goals of hipster parents.

> "They believe becoming a parent should not require one to relinquish creative control over one's life, move to the suburbs, and purchase a minivan. As Ariel Gore, the author of a book entitled *The Hip Mama Survival Guide*, told MSNBC: 'If I'm a punk rocker or I'm really into Hungarian folk dancing . . . and that's who I am, why should I have to leave that behind and raise my kid in some generic middle-class American reality that doesn't feel authentic to me?'"

The article goes on to say,

"This new generation of parents, raised on constant reminders of their own individual uniqueness, refuses to see themselves as merely the latest in a long line of people who have reared children. Because they have so little perspective beyond their own limited experience, their search for authenticity and meaning quickly deteriorates into an orgy of exposure and self-regard. Children are relegated to the role of stagehands in their parents' dramatic transformation from boy to man, girl to woman."[4]

It doesn't take much more than a quick look at Facebook to prove this theory to be true. Parents are posting all manner of quotes and photos of their children that will humiliate those same children ten years down the road, simply to illustrate whatever point the parents are trying to prove.

Don't get us wrong. There are parents who dress hip and think creatively and counterculturally who are not stuck in their own adolescence. But then there are those who fall in line with the philosophies behind Neal Pollack's book *Alternadad: The True Story of One Family's Struggle to Raise a Cool Kid in America*. For some hipster parents, "cool" is valued over character. And these parents are often, unfortunately, living with all of the insecurity that marks the teenage years.

He needs: awareness. Many hipster parents value being "cool" and "in the know." Being a parent, however, often involves being uncool (especially when your kids become teens) and a high degree of uncertainty. When I do an assessment or a first-time appointment with a family, I worry immediately about certain children . . . or maybe I should say, certain parents. These parents walk in wearing the same jeans their children wear, saying the same number of "like's" per sentence, and checking their cell phones just as often. The teenage child of this parent could easily have an identity crisis. Teenagers are supposed to be the hip, edgy ones of the family. If their parent is already taking up that space, they often don't know who to be.

If you are a Hipster Parent, be the Hipster *Parent*. You can still be cool. You can give your child the freedom to be cool as well. But don't make image your highest priority. Don't teach your children to value cool over character. Your children need to respect you more than like you, as Sissy already said. They need you to offer a version of adulthood that makes them look forward to growing up, rather than seeing their adolescence as "the glory years."

Your insecurities will beckon you to pay more attention to your image than to your child. Be aware of him. Be aware of her. Who are your kids becoming? What do they need from you? How can you encourage who they are emotionally, cognitively, and stylistically, rather than who you think they should be? You will not always be "in the know." Parenting requires a certain amount of uncertainty. But you can be certain that your children look to you to help them discover who they are. And you can only offer that to the degree that you know who you are . . . the grown-up, even sometimes uncool version.

The Second-Chance Parent

She is: interdependent. This parent unknowingly sees her daughter's or son's childhood as an extension of her own. Their identities are intertwined—one cannot exist without the other. The second-chance parent can look one of two ways. One sees her daughter as a chance to redeem the mistakes she made while she was growing up. The other sees his child as someone to "follow in his old dad's footsteps."

I recently saw both types of second-chance parents played out. One mother came in for counseling with her fourteen-year-old daughter. "I'm so worried about her. She says she has friends, but I don't think she's happy. I go to events at school and I see the popular girls sitting, talking, and laughing in a group in the middle of everything. But my daughter and a few other girls are usually off to the side. They're much quieter than the others. I just know she's feeling lonely and isolated."

When I brought the daughter back to my office, this insightful teenager said, "I know my mom is worried about me, but I'm fine. I don't really want to be popular. I've figured out that, at my school, the popular girls aren't popular because they're well liked. They're popular because everyone's afraid of them. I don't want to be that. I like my friends." This girl had the same insight as many of the children quoted earlier in this chapter. She understood what her mom wanted, and she knew what she wanted for herself. But what she didn't know was how desperately her mom wanted to be a part of that very same group twenty-five years earlier.

A dad recently picked his ten-year-old son up from our summer camp. Before they left to go home, we walked outside to throw the ball for my dog, Blueberry. Tommy picked up a ball and threw it as hard as he could down the driveway. His dad immediately yelled, "Get your arm straight, Tommy! Keep your eye on the ball." You probably have the same thought I did. He's just throwing the ball for a dog, for crying out loud. But this father played college baseball. He knew how to throw a ball correctly, and he was going to make sure his son did too. He wanted him to have "every opportunity that he had growing up"—which really meant he wanted him to do everything he did, and do it just as well.

She needs: an independent connectedness. Your child will be different from you. Let me say it again: your child will be different from you. I know you know that to be true, but it's sometimes easy to forget. They will be different. They will have different needs, different interests, different hopes, and different dreams. He may want to play a different sport. She may hate music lessons. Your family may be athletic, and she may be the only one who is artistic. Being connected has nothing to do with being alike.

What interests your son or daughter? What is he passionate about? What does she love? Allow her to be her. Allow him to be him. Being a parent involves letting go of who you were or weren't so that your child can simply be. Think about if there are any ways you are unwittingly putting pressure on your child to stand in as your second chance. Your child needs to be independently connected to you in a way that frees you each to be the child and grown-up God uniquely designed you to be.

The Pain-Free Parent

He is: lifeless. The pain-free parent has experienced profound pain at some point in his childhood. He has hurt in a way that he longs to never hurt again. In turn, he has committed to living his life in a way that isolates him from pain. The problem is that, in so doing, he also isolates himself from good.

His father never showed any type of physical affection. To touch his son, to hug him or ruffle his hair, would tap into that pain in a way that would bring back everything he has spent years trying to press down. So he doesn't. He doesn't touch or hug. He doesn't offer the physical affection his son craves.

Her mother shamed her any time she cried as a child. "Why are you crying? There's nothing worth getting that upset about.

You just overreact to everything." She has, in turn, determined to live her life above feelings. "Get over it," she says to herself daily. And so, when her daughter is hurt or rejected, it touches on her feelings of shame and sorrow. But instead of allowing that sadness to emerge, she turns immediately to rage. At least when she's angry, she's still in control.

He needs: vulnerability. Pain is inevitable. You will experience pain. Your children will experience pain. You will feel your children's pain sometimes more than your own. To be a parent is a perpetual lesson in vulnerability. It's not just that you wear your heart on your sleeve; it seems to live there. Your child will bring you tremendous joy and tremendous pain. If you isolate yourself from the emotion that vulnerability brings, you also isolate yourself from your child.

In her book *Plan B*, Anne Lamott wrote, "My friend Mark, who works with church youth groups, reminded me recently that [my teenage son] Sam doesn't need me to correct his feelings. He needs me to listen, to be clear and fair and parental. But most of all he needs me to be alive in a way that makes him feel he will be able to bear adulthood, because he is terrified of death, and that includes growing up to be one of the stressed-out, gray-faced adults he sees rushing around him."[5]

You may be trying to be a pain-free parent. If you are, I would guess it's not working very well. The pain seeps out in fissures of anger and emotion that feels like it could swallow you up. Pain doesn't lessen just because we hold it inside. Much like the fear we talked about earlier, it swells and swells, threatening to burst. And you have to work even harder to push it farther underground.

To face your pain, to bring it into the light and lay it at the

feet of someone you trust, will be one of the biggest gifts you
could ever give your child. In essence, you are giving him you.
You are freeing yourself up to parent with your whole self, rather
than fragmented bits and pieces of lifelessness. Grow up. Grow
up with the tenderness and vulnerability your children long for
from you. They will, in turn, be better prepared to love others
with the same tenderness and vulnerability, which is more commonly referred to as strength.

Which parent do you see yourself most closely resembling?

What do you feel you need in response?

*Where could you give God and others in your community
opportunities to help meet that need?*

Putting the Ways of Childhood Behind

Sissy and David both laugh at me because of my e-mail account.
I will, at times, have more than two thousand e-mails on my
desktop. I've realized it's because I don't understand how to put
them in the right place—in computer language, to archive them.
Instead, I leave them on my working desktop and am reminded
by the little red circle on my mail icon just how many are waiting on me.

Unresolved issues can feel like that little red circle . . .
hounding you to pay attention. In reading this chapter, the number in your red circle may be increasing. You may be more and
more aware of pain and hurt from your past. You may be more

conscious of some ways you've gotten stuck. This chapter is not meant to get you worked up and stressed out over those issues. It is also not meant for you to use it to judge another's parenting. What it is meant to do is help you become aware of the parts of your past that are triggered, and then put them away (archive them) in a place in which they lose their power.

> When I was a child, I talked like a child, I thought like a child, I reasoned like a child. When I became a man, I put the ways of childhood behind me. (1 Cor. 13:11 NIV)

Your past affects your future but doesn't have to define it. It doesn't have to define you as a person, and it doesn't have to define you as a parent. One of the things we tell our counseling groups at Daystar is that nothing in your life is ever so bad that you can't give. As a parent, no pain in your past is ever so bad that you can't love. In fact, all that you need to parent your child is already inside of you, including your pain.

You may struggle with feelings of inadequacy. You may feel an interdependence to your child that tangles the two of you together at times. You may have days when you feel lifeless and weeks where fear greets you at every turn. In fact, you probably will feel all of these things—at least a little.

Be aware of your past, but parent in the present. You can do this by processing what triggers you with someone you trust, whether it's your spouse, a friend, or a counselor. Journaling can help. Write out your thoughts and feelings to God. God can use your pain and all you have learned from it to give you more courage, wisdom, and even hope on this great parenting journey.

The process of growing older is not necessarily allied to growing wickeder, though the two do often happen together. Children are meant to grow up, and not to become Peter Pans. Not to lose innocence and wonder, but to proceed on the appointed journey; that journey upon which it is certainly not better to travel hopefully than to arrive, though we must travel hopefully if we are to arrive.[6]

Traveling hopefully is what growing up is all about. Neither you nor I, our spouses, nor even our parents have arrived yet. We haven't become all that we will be. As 1 Corinthians 13 goes on to say, "We don't yet see things clearly. We're squinting in a fog, peering through a mist. But it won't be long before the weather clears and the sun shines bright! We'll see it all then, see it all as clearly as God sees us, knowing him directly just as he knows us!" (v. 12 MSG)

In the meantime, our past will still be triggered by our present. But we can be bigger than the pall cast from our collective childhoods, with God's help. We can do what our children long for us to do: grow up in a way that makes being a grown-up look like a glorious adventure.

4.

Being a Balanced Parent

—with David

DESPITE OUR BEST ATTEMPTS AT HALTING HER growth, my daughter turned six, and it became painfully evident that we should send her to school at some point before she turned twenty. After much research, we enrolled her in our neighborhood school. Summer came to a close, ushering in the beginning of a new school year. I can still remember day one and dropping off this delicate little creature that I loved with every fiber of my being. Interestingly enough, week three stands out in my mind with even greater clarity.

The beginning of week two announced a letter from the principal. The kindergarten parents received a note in their child's folder that read something like this:

59

Dear Parents,

We've had a wonderful first week of school. Your child is settling into the routine of the kindergarten year, building familiarity with the classroom, learning the rhythm of the school day, and getting to know his/her teacher and many new friends. We remain encouraged by the new and exciting events taking place in the learning environment. Thank you for your support and partnership.

We invite you to join us in supporting independence in your student. Beginning week three, you will drop off through the carpool line; your child will walk into the building independently and find their way to the classroom. We know you will find this arrival plan to benefit your son/daughter as well as facilitating an efficient beginning to our school day.

Many thanks,
The Elementary Faculty
and Administration

I found this to be the kindest way anyone could have possibly said, "Get out of the building, kindergarten parents. The fact that you are hovering and lingering isn't helping anyone. We're giving you one more week, and then we're cutting the umbilical cord."

We spent week two practicing navigating the hallways so my daughter could identify and master a path from the parking lot to her current classroom. My sweet daughter is—how shall we say it?—*navigationally challenged*. What comes naturally to the spatially strong males in her classroom doesn't come naturally to her. She turned left when she should have turned right;

she headed toward the second-grade hall rather than the kinder-garten hall, and even passed her classroom on one attempt. We kept practicing and eventually found our way to her classroom seconds before the bell rang, on day four.

Week three rolled around and I woke that morning with a pit in my stomach. Everything in me wanted to be about "support-ing independence" and celebrating this baby step of opportunity for my little girl, but I was plagued with fear. I'll finish setting the stage for that magical Monday by also saying that my sweet daughter had fallen in love with Mrs. Knight, her delightful kin-dergarten teacher, and had requested at bedtime the night before that we make muffins to bring her this day. My wife woke early and assembled the mix and lined the muffin tins. Lily helped pour mix into each slot and watched with anticipation as they rose, baked, and cooled on a tray before arranging them on a plate with great care.

I was busy loading the car with books and supplies for a class I'd be teaching that morning in the home of one of our board members. I'd called ahead to say that I'd arrive just after drop-off to help move chairs and transform her beautiful, spa-cious home into a lecture hall. Knowing I'd be setting up and moving furniture, I only half dressed. I hung a starched shirt and tie in the back of the car and headed out wearing only kha-kis and an undershirt, with plans to finish dressing later. After all, I was "supporting independence" today and wouldn't be get-ting out of the car anyhow.

We loaded her backpack and the sacred plate of carefully placed muffins, and headed off to school. As we drove, I said something like, "You are such a big girl, walking yourself into school today for the first time." I went on to convince her that she had it down and was going to have a fantastic day. (I was secretly convincing myself.) When we pulled into the drop-off line, I said a prayer for her day, kissed her cheek, watched her wiggle her backpack onto her shoulders, and handed off the plate of muffins. Just as I finished, the principal opened the car door and greeted her by name, and I watched as she stepped toward the front door, seeing nothing but this little blonde ponytail dangling over this massive pink backpack, tiny little legs spilling out the bottom. I swallowed hard and put the car back in drive.

I moved forward and prayed something like, "God, I really need You to come through this time. Please help her find her way there safely." I made it to the edge of the campus, swallowed hard again . . . and then I wheeled that car into the parking lot faster than an ambulance enters the ER bay. I leaped out of the car and began running like a madman across the lawn.

I wanted so badly to trust that she'd make two lefts and a right and find her way there, but I was disintegrating—swimming in fear. I envisioned her making two rights and then a left, ending up in the fourth-grade hall, drowning in panic. She'd drop the muffins on the ground and the fourth-grade boys would begin using them as Hacky Sacks. She'd be paralyzed, and still working out this memory in therapy as an adult.

I didn't want her to see evidence of my lack of trust. I didn't need to go inside the school; I just needed to know that she made it safely to her classroom. So, I began scaling the side of the building, looking inside every window, trying desperately to find her.

What would be going through your mind if you saw a desperate-looking man peeping in the windows of an elementary school, sweaty and dressed in an undershirt? Yes, I'd call the police and identify the pedophile myself.

I was completely unaware of myself in this moment. Anxiety and fear had hijacked any semblance of rational thinking, and I was responding without reason. I made my way to the last window and looked inside just as my daughter was rounding the corner successfully into her classroom. I saw Mrs. Knight smile and reach down to hug her as she handed over the muffins with pride, her face just beaming. I slithered down the side of the building and headed to the car. I closed the door, gripped the wheel, and burst into tears.

Nothing about sending kids we love out into the world feels natural to us as parents. We know in our heads that it's the right thing to do, but nothing about it feels instinctive or familiar. I talk often with moms about the balance of being safe and letting go. Gina Bria, an anthropologist, wrote a book called *The Art of Family*, and she said this about her sons:

> The work of mothering a son is mostly about stepping aside with precise timing. I want my sons, both of them, to learn from me that they are free to be rooted in home and still be abroad in the world as men.[1]

Free to be rooted in home is the "being safe." Being abroad in the world is the "letting go." The balance is in loving them, protecting them, and keeping them safe, while also releasing them into the world and supporting independence. It's easier said than done.

Within this chapter, we'll take a look at balance—balancing love and fear, discipline and relationship, boundaries and freedom. We'll consider how to be people *with* emotions rather than parenting *out* of emotion. We'll discuss balancing opportunities for activity and experience (sports, dance, art), while also balancing time together as a family. We'll examine balancing support, like helping your child with homework, while reinforcing the idea of becoming an independent learner.

Balancing Love and Fear

Earlier I shared the story of two parents dropping off their son for college and responding out of love and fear. Parenting is a long, slow journey of experiencing the two and responding more out of one than the other. Throw in the towel on dodging fear; it's part of the game. The question becomes, how can I operate in the presence of fear, acknowledge that it exists, yet not parent out of that place?

We believe the only way to parent out of love in the presence of fear is simply to pray that the truth of 2 Timothy 1:12 would become more and more real to you as you go forward. "I know the One I have believed in and am persuaded that He is able to guard what has been entrusted to me until that day" (HCSB). Pray to believe that God will protect what He has entrusted to you. We live in the context of a larger story. We can only see what is taking place within the story we are living, with occasional glances into the larger story.

Going back to my story of my daughter and the muffins, just try to get out of the parking lot. Avoid going back into the building when you can. Find ways to engage in small moments of supporting independence, and be vocal about how much you believe in who your kids are and who they are becoming.

✗ *Where are you most afraid as a parent?*

Identify an area where you could stop gripping and invite more trust.

Balancing Discipline and Relationship

Let's think more about the words of "what He has entrusted." This means God specifically called me into the role of parenting Lily, Baker, and Witt. He didn't call another man to father them, but *this* man. Believing that means that I'm called to step more into my role with intention and purpose. It means that I'm called to care for these three lives—to protect and steward these gifts.

One of the ways we steward and protect our kids is with discipline. We are asked about discipline in our offices on a daily basis, as well as about every time we speak on parenting. The topic of discipline generates a plethora of questions, a range of emotions, and a variety of opinions. We often get stuck on the *mechanics* of disciplining kids and lose the *purpose* of discipline. *The Message* translates Proverbs 13:24 this way: "A refusal to correct is a refusal to love; love your children by disciplining them." Discipline has always been intended for teaching, shaping, and protecting our kids. The purpose of disciplining our children is to teach them as a means of loving them. Furthermore, if discipline is designed as a means of loving our children, our posture in discipline should be one of love, not of anger. Discipline should never be about harming or shaming our children.

We've all heard the old sayings that rules without relationship lead to rebellion, but we'd add that relationship without any rules leads to kids feeling too much power and a lack of safety. The goal is to work toward having rules and relationship in place, and to parent consistently with both.

Identify an area where you want to be more consistent in enforcing consequences.

Consider becoming more comfortable with saying, "I'm OK with that not making sense to you," or "I'm comfortable with you being angry about that consequence."

Balancing Boundaries and Freedom

This need most often shows up in our attempts to set healthy boundaries while also supporting our kids' independence and allowing them to have freedom. You'll see this in our conversations about the importance of allowing kids to struggle. Tim Kimmel calls them "designed dilemmas," and the folks at Love and Logic call them SLOs (Significant Learning Opportunities). They are simply moments when we avoid jumping in and rescuing, and instead we allow our kids to learn through their decisions (good and bad). These moments are always about developing character and strengthening resilience.

As I write this, my own sons are in a lazy season of responsibility. I commented to them yesterday that it confuses me how two guys who are so skilled in hitting free throws can't seem to hit the laundry basket. I find their dirty clothes and wet towels scattered throughout our house, sometimes in their rooms, sometimes beside the shower, and sometimes lying on the laundry room floor, inches away from the dirty clothes basket. Really?

I find their backpacks and soccer cleats lying *in front* of the lockers of our house, not *in* the lockers. I find their empty plates *beside* the dishwasher, not *in* it. And it's not uncommon to find they've relieved themselves in the toilet but for some reason missed that step of flushing the evidence. Almost there, but not quite.

Yesterday they packed their soccer shorts, jerseys, balls, cleats, and equipment and set it by the front door to take for an after-school practice. As I left for work, I noticed it was still by the door; they'd been gone for over an hour. This is the equivalent of remembering to do your homework and forgetting to turn it in. I looked down at my phone to find a text from one of my sons asking if I could drop it off at school en route to work.

I paused to consider my options. Technically, I could have pulled it off. I had just enough time to make the drop and still make it to my first appointment, but I opted not to. Instead, I contacted my wife and we corporately agreed to use this opportunity to strengthen the responsibility muscle that has been underworked lately. I shot an e-mail to their coach to let him know that my boys would show up at practice today in their school uniforms, with no equipment, and that we would require them to extend an apology for showing up unprepared, which is disrespectful to the time their coach gives to the team. We also wanted to free him up to handle them however he chose to handle players who came unprepared to practice. We are hoping this involves some sort of running laps, acting as water boys, or giving back to the team.

It seems important to note that the conversation with my wife included discussion about what we'd likely encounter on the other side of this parenting decision. We aren't operating under the illusion that our sons will enter the house with a sense of gratitude for the learning experience they were handed. In the face of failure or disappointment, boys more often blame others rather than take personal responsibility. Girls tend to blame themselves; boys blame others.

That's exactly what stepped into the sliding door of the van—sweaty, angry, blaming boys. They were mad at themselves, but preferred to blame my wife. She first responded with empathy and tried to acknowledge how hard it must have been to show up at practice unprepared, not knowing how it would be handled. One of my sons spewed his venom on her and accused the two of us of being uncaring for not bringing the equipment to school. She calmly reminded them that she didn't pack the equipment; neither did she leave it sitting by the door. She responded with empathy again and then turned on some music to drown out the drama.

There's nothing else that needs to be said, though we often do in these moments. We take away from the rich understanding that takes place when our kids learn through experience with boundaries and consequences. We too often dilute the learning with a lecture (more on this later).

Identify an area where you'd like to support independence through allowing freedom and letting your son/daughter learn through a decision.

Balancing Emotion

Another gift we give as balanced parents is having emotion but not parenting out of emotion. As my sons were spewing their venom, my wife had thoughts of saying and doing things she'd later regret. Speaking and acting during emotionally charged moments with our kids is almost always a mistake. Our kids are better served by hearing us say something like "I'm going to take a break" or "We both need some space." Time-outs aren't just for two-year-olds. They are for kids and adults of all ages. Taking a break is a way of creating the space you need as a parent to respond with empathy, respect, and wisdom. Parenting out of emotion is a little bit like going grocery shopping on an empty stomach. We almost always end up making impulsive, less-than-thoughtful decisions that we later regret. Taking a break allows us to step away and consider if discipline needs to be a part of the equation, and if so, how to do that and let it be about instruction and not emotion.

Balancing emotion also means learning to respond (or not respond) while keeping yourself in check. A mom I enjoy and respect shared a story of her middle school son disrespecting her one morning. He woke up grumpy, as is not uncommon with a fourteen-year-old boy. He snapped at her when she poked her head in his bedroom to remind him that he'd hit snooze four times and they were leaving in thirty minutes whether he was ready or not. He got up, dressed, and came into the kitchen. He snapped for the second time about the breakfast options. She reminded her grumpy, sulky son that if he continued to speak disrespectfully to her, she'd leave him at home and he could walk to school that morning. He backed down temporarily but was obviously simmering below the surface.

On the way to school, he erupted like a volcano. He pro-
voked his sister, barked at his mom from the backseat, and was
making threats. His mother reminded him that she had chosen
not to get fully dressed yet as she was going back home to get
ready for an event she had mid-morning. She said, "I'm wearing my pajamas and a terrycloth robe. If you speak one more
disrespectful word to someone in this car, I'll remind you that I
am confident enough in myself to march into school with you,
find your baseball coach, and tell him that you won't be staying
for practice this afternoon because baseball is an extracurricular
activity, something supported in response to his respect of family and giving him that opportunity, not a requirement."

Put a point on the scoreboard for Team Mom. He backed
down at the idea of her entering the school building in her pj's
and searching the hallways for his coach.

Weeks later, he woke again, his body and mind having been
kidnapped overnight. *Invasion of the Body Snatchers*, part two.
He conveniently seems to choose the mornings when his dad
leaves early for work. He started the day barking orders, making
demands, and polluting the atmosphere of their home. This day
he announced that he wasn't going to school and no one could
make him. His mother responded by saying, "You're right. I can't
make you go to school, but if you aren't sick, I will call the school
and tell them you aren't. It is an unexcused absence, and they
may report you as being truant."

He snapped back with something smart-aleck like, "You'd
turn your own son over, wouldn't you?" She said, "Actually if
you're doing something illegal, I would." He then played a wild
card and grabbed her phone. He acted as if he was going to
smash it on the floor. She reached to grab his arm and scratched

him by accident. He acted as if she'd cut him with a switchblade and began writhing in pain. He started yelling, "I'm calling the police on you. I'm going to tell them you hurt me on purpose."

He ran to grab the house phone and began dialing 911. Everything in her wanted to grab the phone out of his hand (and pop him with it). She resisted, realizing what grabbing had accomplished moments ago. She simply said, "Go right ahead and call. I could use the support."

As the operator answered and began to ask questions, the boy screamed and slammed down the phone. Inevitably, this type of desperation signaled the police. Within ten minutes, they had dispatched the police and an officer was knocking on the door. The boy answered the door and the officer inquired if they needed assistance. The boy immediately said, "No, everything is fine." The mom surfaced behind him and said, "No, actually it's not, Officer. We need your help."

The boy looked like he might wet himself at this point, and the mom invited the officer in. She retold the story in his presence and asked for guidance. The officer, sensing this was a smart, well-intentioned, great mom, said, "Son, sit down, and we're going to talk."

The next thing she remembers is the police officer yelling and reminding the boy that a parent could call for something as minor as a teenager refusing to do his homework when asked and could file an unruly petition. The boy was in tears by this point. The mom enjoyed a second cup of coffee.

Identify an activity or a place where you can go when you feel emotionally charged and need some time/space to make more thoughtful parenting decisions.

Balancing Time

In the chapter on being an intentional parent, you were invited to consider doing a time/activity assessment to put a magnifying glass to the ways you spend time as a family, and to dissect the amount of time you spend doing the activities you do as a family. The challenge was to see how this aligned (or didn't align) with your mission or core values. This basic exercise can have some surprising results. I love hearing from families who've attempted this, and learning the strategic, creative ways they choose to adjust the rhythm of their families. One family chose to turn an annual spring break trip into a staycation and opportunities for service. They alternated days and would explore a different part of the city on one day and serve in some capacity on the following day. Their children were actively involved in developing the structure of that time.

Another family committed to take one Saturday of each sport season and sacrifice being at a game to volunteer as a family. This decision felt important in communicating to their kids that while they valued sports and the extracurricular experiences their children had been given, they would sacrifice that experience at different intervals to prioritize service. As their kids got older, the stakes got higher in missing games, yet maintaining this commitment rooted this family in a decision that best maintained congruence with their family mission.

A family I worked with banned travel sports. They had two children and realized that they spent more weekends divided than together, more weekends in hotels of other cities than in their own home, and more time with other families than their own. While they parented some gifted athletes and realized they were sacrificing some opportunity down the road by limiting involvement in this way, they chose to pursue only recreational leagues and school sports opportunities.

A simple decision we've made as a family is to periodically host what we call "home church." While we believe strongly in corporate worship and remain grateful for our local church, my travel with speaking seasonally means I may be gone two out of four weekends in a month. Because I work several evenings with my practice, I could go for multiple days during a week and miss the afternoon/evening ritual of being with my kids. I'd then board a plane on a Friday and spend the weekend speaking out of state on Friday and Saturday. Sunday becomes the only day to really see my family. Rather than heading out of the house on Sunday morning, we host "home church." We break bread together over a big pancake breakfast in our pj's. Breakfast is followed by my kids plotting a service together between the three of them, while my wife and I catch up on conversations we've missed over the week.

We started this tradition when our kids were barely in school. My children have this opportunity to work together and plan something that allows our family to worship together. When they were young, they would line the living room with American Girl dolls, stuffed animals, and action figures. Sometimes they would each be given a nickel or dime to place in the offering plate. Even the dog was given something to tithe.

My kids have come in costume and acted out a skit that connects to the "message." They've performed solos, read from the *Jesus Storybook Bible*; we experience God in the safety of our home. I wish I had recorded these "services" over the years—hearing my children read scripture aloud, my daughter read something she learned from her journal, my sons play guitar, or one of them pray for our family. I have so many rich memories of this slow, sweet time between the walls of our home. One Sunday we hiked together and pointed out evidence of where we saw God in nature.

These times have allowed us to balance family and activity, in addition to the opportunities for my kids to creatively work together and the chance to build connection among the five of us (six counting the dog).

We live in a culture that elevates activity and opportunity above connection. We value fast above slow, more above less, performance above presence. There's never been a time when it's been harder to slow down, build connection, value time together, linger as a family, and create simple memories.

Have each member of your family write down his or her idea of a perfect Saturday and drop that slip of paper into a hat. Read them aloud together and decide what you'd like to do with the ideas.

Balancing Support

Another area to emphasize is balancing support. Throughout their development, kids need support—emotional support, relational support, physical support, spiritual support, and academic support. As you study your daughter/son, you will identify areas where she/he will need more support than in others. The real question is how much support to give. It's important to offer enough support but not so much that you hinder their development.

An area in which we tend to offer too much support to girls is relational support. Moms and dads can step into the trap of problem solving for girls in the face of relational challenges—a friend betrays them, a boyfriend acts like a jerk, a group excludes them. We step into these moments with statements like "You need to tell her to . . ." or "Next time, just . . ." or "Don't let her . . ." Being there to listen is so important, but giving unsolicited advice can send a message to a girl that she isn't smart, strong, or creative enough to navigate these complicated relational hurdles herself.

A number of boys need additional academic support. The compulsory model of schooling we use in our country is heavy on verbal and written expression, and it involves a lot of sitting still and auditory instruction. None of these play to a boy's strengths. School can be a challenging environment for boys. If his learning profile includes any gaps or areas of deficit, the equation simply gets that much more complicated. Without being aware or ever intending to do so, we can train a boy to believe that he can't navigate his academic world without consistent support and intervention. This can start with parents who camp out at the kitchen table beside a boy when he attempts homework. The message here is, "You aren't smart, strategic, organized, or motivated enough to do the work on your own." He'd be better served to be seated in proximity while you attend to another task (cooking dinner, paying bills, returning e-mails, or so on) and he attends to his own work. You are available for questions or to help in places where he gets stuck, but you are not there to do his work for him or prompt him through his own work. The long goal is that he become an independent learner.

I've officially lost count of the number of young men who were bright or brilliant, some valedictorians, salutatorians, and merit scholars, who managed to flunk themselves out of school within one to two semesters because they never learned how to be independent learners. Unless someone was standing over them, checking a planner, looking online at assignments, helping finish assignments, prompting, redirecting, or finishing work, they had no idea how to operate independently. This made being a student at college a difficult, almost impossible task.

Equally important is to identify where we could begin nurturing greater independence in multiple areas of our kids' lives—folding their own laundry, preparing their own lunches, paying their own car insurance, managing their own spending, and the list goes on and on.

> *Two amazing questions to ask kids are "What are you thinking?" and "What are you going to do in response to that?" Take small steps to shift the ownership back to your son/daughter as a way of nurturing independence, creativity, resilience, and resourcefulness.*

5.

Being a Consistent Parent

—with Sissy

"IT'S JUST NOT NATURAL TO BE A GOOD, KIND parent." The mother who said these words to us at a recent mother/daughter event seemed good and kind to us. She was a well-educated, well-respected physician in her community, but she was having a hard time parenting her fourteen-year-old daughter. "It's just not natural," she repeated again with growing emphasis. "What's natural for me is to be angry, frustrated, and inconsistent. I try one thing and it doesn't work. So then I try something else. I just wish there was some kind of manual. Parenting is harder than anyone ever tells you. I mean, they come into the world crying, after all. That should be some kind of sign as to what's to come."

You may have felt the same way. (You probably do often

if you have a fourteen-year-old.) You come up with a plan for chores around the house. Maybe even get inspired and create a color-coded chart. It works beautifully for a couple of weeks. But then Christmas rolls around. Things get busy, and it's easier to get your husband to take the trash out than it is to hound your son. Your daughter doesn't have time to clean her room, and your in-laws will be here soon, so you might as well do it this one time. One time turns into several, and soon the chart is gathering dust.

You decide you are going to teach your children about healthy eating. You make a trip to Whole Foods and stock the pantry with veggie sticks and vitamin water. Everyone's on board and excited, until Wednesday, when soccer practice runs long and lets out just a few minutes before church. The only way to find time for dinner is to stop by Sonic on the way. And all of a sudden, what started as a "we'll get back on track tomorrow" becomes a regular convenience in a busy schedule.

Inconsistency happens. There is no way to avoid it as a person and maybe, especially, as a parent. Aldous Huxley said, "Consistency is contrary to nature, contrary to life. The only completely consistent people are the dead."[1] Or, as our doctor-mom friend would say, "It's just not natural."

But all of the "parenting experts" say consistency is important. Obviously, we do as well. Out of all of the parenting characteristics we could include in this book, it is one of the twelve we have chosen because we believe it is one of the most important, but also because we see parents struggle with consistency every day. Maybe they struggle because they really don't know how to start. Maybe they struggle because they don't know how to stop the busyness of their lives long enough to establish a pattern of consistency. That's what we're really talking about in this chapter—creating a pattern. You are going to struggle. You're going to stop by Sonic and take the trash out for your son. You will get angry with your daughter, and you won't follow through on your discipline. But you can still establish a pattern of consistency in your home. And we want this chapter to help give you a place to start.

Why is consistency so important? It's fun to be flexible, and consistency can squash spontaneity in your family. Yes, it can—on both counts. Spontaneity and flexibility are important, and fun is vital to the life and health of your family. In fact, we've got a whole chapter devoted to that, chapter 6, "Being a Playful Parent." But consistency creates a sense of security for children. It helps them feel safe, grounded. Children crave predictability, and in an age where childhood anxiety is being referred to as an epidemic, predictability and consistency are maybe more important than ever. Teenagers, likewise, crave consistency, even though they may not say it out loud. They need consistent consequences to give them opportunities to both learn from their mistakes and enhance their self worth.

We've broken down this chapter into the three areas in which we believe consistency is most important: values, responsibilities, and discipline. In each section, we'll discuss tips on how to implement each. But they'll only work when you, as a parent, are consistent. Consistency isn't easy. However, it's a battle that we believe is worth fighting. And it can create a pattern that will lend itself not only to greater security in your children but also to more peace in your home.

Consistent Values

When you think about the way your parents raised you, what did they value? Faith? Financial security? Appearance? Honesty? Try to come up with three of the values that were foundational to your home growing up. (Seriously. We want you to stop reading and come up with three; it's kind of like counseling homework.)

> What were the three most important values in your home when you were growing up?

Now, how did your parents communicate those values to you? Did they teach you directly about them? Was it in the choices they made? Was it by the time you spent focused on those ideals? We would guess it was mainly through those three avenues: words, actions, and time.

If your son or daughter were sitting in my office and I asked him or her the same questions, what would he or she say?

What would your child believe your values to be?

What values do your words reflect (and not just your intentions)?

What about your time?

What about the way you live your life?

You may already be a big-picture person and have thought through your own top three values you want to be foundational to your home. But if you haven't, we would suggest you spend some time on the idea. Talk to your spouse. If you're a single parent, talk to a trusted friend, counselor, or pastor and have that individual help you come up with a list. Maybe even a top ten list. But rank them in order, as best you can.

Next, brainstorm ways you can consistently communicate these values.

David talked in chapter 1 about being intentional. Instilling these values in your children will take intentionality as well, from the time your children are toddlers.

Toddlers and Values

In the toddler years, the majority of your teaching is direct. "Find their eyes," you may say to your three-year-old daughter when she meets someone new, if manners is one of your top ten. "Find their eyes" is a great example, as a matter of fact, of one of the important ways to communicate your values to toddlers. They are learning volumes in this stage, and your consistency is the best teacher. Here are a few more examples of ways to consistently communicate your family values:

USE KEY PHRASES THAT ARE REPETITIVE AND SHORT. "Find their eyes," "Say Please," and "No touch" are great examples. They will be more likely to pay attention because of the brevity, and more likely to remember because of the repetition.

TEACH USING VISUALS. In Melissa's and my book *Modern Parents, Vintage Values*, we give an illustration of teaching compassion to children using Colossians 3:12 and putting it on as they're getting dressed and undressed for the day.[2] With toddlers, you could have them draw a picture of a shoe and write *compassion* on the paper.

START MODELING THE VALUES NOW THAT YOU WANT YOUR CHILDREN TO GROW UP WITH. It's not too early to take them with you to a sick friend's house. They can draw a picture on a birthday card you're sending. Give them chances to be a part of the choices you make that reflect your values.

EXPLAIN YOUR CHOICES. Your toddler will watch you a great deal, but they often won't understand the whys behind your actions. Before you walk out the door to Bible study, tell your daughter, "Mommy is going to learn more about Jesus." Let your son see the picture of the boy you're sponsoring in Haiti and tell him why.

GIVE YOUR PRIORITIES PRIORITY TIME. Some priorities, in these years, will be easier than others. If family time is something you want your family to value, you will likely have a great deal of that when your children are toddlers. Other timing choices, however, can be a little less convenient. Church, for example, can be difficult: the effort it takes to get them up, dressed, and out the door can make you wonder at times if it's worth it. It is . . . as are the other choices you make as a family that may be difficult now, but, as a result, will more easily become habits in the future.

PRAISE, PRAISE, PRAISE! At this age, your child wants desperately to please you. Kids hear your approval or disapproval in your voice and see it in your eyes. Take every opportunity to reinforce and encourage positive values in their behavior. It will make them want to repeat the scenario to please you more.

As basic as it sounds, toddlers need to know why you value the things you do. They need you to teach them directly and explain the choices you make. And they need you to consistently carry those same values into their childhood years.

Children and Values

Childhood is a rich time of learning. In *Wild Things*, David and Stephen call a boy between the ages of five and eight "The Lover."[3] In *Raising Girls*, we talk about girls from six to ten as

being in the "Adventurous Years," with one of the primary characteristics being their responsiveness.[4] They continue to want
to please you, as their parents, and they have a much greater
capacity for understanding and responding to truth than in their
toddler years. As a result, they are ripe and ready for learning
what your family values.

BE CONCRETE. Jean Piaget, a pioneer in the field of
psychology, called this stage of development the Concrete
Operational Stage.

> The child thinks in terms of concrete, existing objects. He
> is able to conserve, order, classify, but does not hypoth-
> esize or use abstractions. It is the third stage of intellectual
> development in which the child is not yet ready to address
> "possibilities," but attends only to the given objects and fig-
> ures in its environment.[5]

So, for example, your son just hit his little sister. To be concrete would be to say, "Kind little boys do not hit their sisters"
and take him to time-out. Saying, "What would it mean for you
to be kind to your sister the next time this happens?" will only
confuse him. In order to teach him in these years, it is imperative that we understand and speak in the way he learns.

THINK LITERALLY ABOUT YOUR OWN ACTIONS.
As we have already said, their thinking is concrete. What applies
to one applies to all, and that all includes you. When you are
teaching them honesty and tell a friend on the phone you can't
get together because you have plans when you don't, you have
broken that rule. You are their hero and the person they want
most to be like. You're going to blow it at times. But, remember,

we're talking about a pattern. And your children desperately want you to be all that they already believe you are.

MAKE IT FUN. Children love an adventure. At our summer camp, we took the second through fourth graders to a tearoom to show off the manners they had been learning. In *Modern Parents, Vintage Values*, we end each chapter with an experience to reinforce the values parents are trying to teach. What kind of experience could you create with your child that would reinforce the words you are using with action and with fun?

FOCUS ON THE POSITIVE. I recently met with a mom and her third-grade daughter. Almost every sentence the mom said centered on what her daughter was doing wrong. "You told me you didn't have any homework." "You didn't clean your room when I asked you to." As her mom went through the laundry list of offenses, her daughter's eyes eventually glazed over. Again, they want to please you in these years. They are discouraged when they fail and can become hopeless when the failure is repetitive. Point out the positive—consistently. Tell your child when he or she makes choices that reflect the values you are trying to teach. You'll reinforce those values and strengthen your relationship as well.

GIVE THEM OPPORTUNITIES TO BE INVOLVED, HOWEVER SMALL. Let your children be a part of your actions that reflect your values. For example, in Nashville, we have a newspaper called the *Contributor*. Homeless and formerly homeless individuals buy the newspapers and sell them on street corners for income. Rather than just buying a newspaper yourself, you could hand your child the money to hand to the vendor. See the difference? If you adopt a family for Christmas, have your children buy the gifts for the children. If you're having a quiet time, see if your daughter wants to get her Bible and read beside you. They want to please you. They also want to have time with you, which will change in the next stage of their development. Use this time as an extra opportunity to teach values.

SET ASIDE THE TIME. When we were growing up, we had plenty of time after school to ride bikes and play outside. Now, it seems as if that kind of free time is in short supply. Between lessons and practices, school evenings are booked up for most families. And then there are the travel sports that drain the weekends. You may have to choose between great activities to create time that reflects your values. We know families who commit to one night a week when no one has any activities other than to be with the family. We know families who choose one sport per season. Whatever you have to do, your children need time to decompress. If you want them to learn the values important to your family, they need you to make that learning time a predictable priority.

Teenagers and Values

A few weeks ago, I met with a sixteen-year-old who had just lost her cell phone privileges. She had lost Facebook as well. When I spoke with her mom, she told me why. Her daughter had been sending inappropriate pictures of herself to several of the boys in her class. In my opinion, the consequences her parents had implemented seemed appropriate and fair. But then her mom went on to say, "This whole thing has made us reevaluate what we want to be like as a family. We're not going to do the Facebook thing. It's just not for our family. Texting either. When she's eighteen, she can do both. But for now, we will just not be a family who texts or uses Facebook." And with that decision on what their family values, her parents cut off the two primary modes of communication that all teenagers use today.

Teaching teenagers values requires a new type of consistency. Choosing your battles becomes profoundly important. Giving kids the opportunity to learn their values themselves, which involves having chances to fail, is also important. Being a consistent parent requires even more creativity (and maybe tenacity) than ever before.

USE THE BACK DOOR. The first sentence of our book *The Back Door to Your Teen's Heart* is, "To the degree that kids can predict you, they will dismiss you."[6] By this point in your life with your teenagers, they think that, pretty much as soon as you open your mouth, they know what you're going to say. And face it: we do get a little more predictable as we get older. When you teach values directly, as we've been encouraging you to do up to this point, you use the front door. "I have talked to you before about being a responsible member of this household. You act like you don't think anyone else lives here and I'm just your maid." Front door. How do those sentences go over with your teenager? Does she respond with, "Thanks Mom; that was really helpful"? We would guess not. A back-door approach would be to walk in the room, let her see you look at her things lying around, and say, "Responsible kids get to hang out with their friends on the weekend." And then walk out of the room and let her wonder. Teach with your actions and with consequences, which we'll talk more about in a few pages.

SAY AS MUCH AS YOU CAN WITH AS FEW WORDS AS YOU CAN. I meet with a lot of moms and adolescent girls at Daystar. I can't even begin to count the number of times I've watched girls dismiss their moms in my office. If you have a teenage daughter, you've felt it yourself. I've seen a lot of girls who've perfected the art of staring toward their moms and uh-huhing enough to look like they're listening. But they've usually stopped after the first sentence. What happens is, because they haven't acknowledged you, you keep going. One of the main complaints of teenagers is how often their parents repeat themselves. It makes sense. But we would encourage you not to wait for an acknowledgment from them. Make your words count. I work with moms on this one a lot. We women are verbal creatures, and that works against us with teens. You're trying to explain, but she only hears it as a lecture. Don't lecture and don't repeat yourself. Try to compact your thoughts into one or two sentences and then make yourself stop.

ASK THEM QUESTIONS. It is vital for teenagers to learn to think for themselves. They need to develop their own faith and their own values. You have spent years teaching them directly. Much of your teaching now comes through opportunities for them to make mistakes. It also comes through questions. If you watch an important movie together, ask them what they learned from the movie rather than speaking first. If your son goes on a mission trip, ask him what he learned about himself and about God. Learn to ask good questions to teach them to think for themselves, rather than thinking for them. Opportunities to think and learn for themselves is what helps teenagers take the values they've learned and make them their own.

RESPECT THEIR VALUES . . . AT LEAST THE ONES THAT ARE RESPECTABLE. When you see your son make a good decision, when he's honest or compassionate, tell him. He still wants to please you, but how that translates in adolescence is that he wants your respect. It helps him respect himself.

DON'T BE AFRAID TO FAIL. We've used the word *pattern* several times throughout this chapter. You're working toward a big-picture consistency, but you are going to be inconsistent. As you try to teach values and walk them out in your own choices, you will fail. It may be that you lose your temper, that you forget an important game, or that you make a mistake that has far-reaching consequences. Your teenagers will often catch these failures. In this stage of life, they are capable of abstract thought. They see you as a person and not just as a parent. Give them an opportunity to learn grace from you. Apologize. Ask for their forgiveness and let them know it's important to ask for and receive God's. In these years, they're hyperaware of their own failures too. Your honesty and integrity in your failures will help them accept themselves and know Christ better in theirs.

HAVE REALISTIC EXPECTATIONS ON THEIR TIME. Teenagers want to be with their friends. It's universal. It's not personal. After nineteen years of counseling children and teens, I've seen it across the board. She will often or even almost always choose her friends over her family, given the choice. But that doesn't mean you give in every time. Just last week, I talked with a family about choosing one block of time on the weekend to set aside as family time. It could be a day or night. The rest of the time, this high school junior wanted to be with her friends. Set more parameters on their time if they're younger, and then widen those with each year.

GIVE THEM OPPORTUNITIES TO EXPERIENCE YOUR VALUES, TOGETHER AND SEPARATELY. Go on mission trips as a family. Serve at a soup kitchen together. Continue to participate in activities that reflect your values as a family unit. And then let her go on a mission trip with her church group.

Give him an opportunity to volunteer with underprivileged children. It has more power if it's your teenager's choice, but you can require your teens to participate on their own in some type of service activity.

USE THE POWER OF PEERS TO REINFORCE YOUR FAMILY VALUES. As teenagers get older, the voices of their peers become louder, while yours often becomes quieter. Use those voices. Whether it's with a church group, FCA, or even a counseling group, they need to consistently connect with other kids who are a positive influence.

We spend a lot of time with parents talking about what normal development looks like, especially for teenagers. One mom recently told us that just the phrase "Narcissistic Years"[7] got her through her daughter's teenage years. (The Narcissistic Years is what we call ages twelve to fifteen for girls. Boys are much the same.) Being consistent in instilling values in your teenagers will feel like an uphill task. You will often be the last to see the changes or the positive choices they make. But don't lose heart . . . or hope.

> So let's not allow ourselves to get fatigued doing good. At the right time we will harvest a good crop if we don't give up, or quit. Right now, therefore, every time we get the chance, let us work for the benefit of all, starting with the people closest to us in the community of faith. (Gal. 6:9–10 MSG)

"At the right time" may still be a few months or years away. They do emerge from teenagedom eventually, but in the meantime, you can think of your children as the people literally closest to you in the community of faith. Keep consistently working for the benefit of all, including your narcissistic teens.

A Few Value-able Examples

To spur on your thinking a little more, we wanted to give some examples of values that we value, as counselors who work with families. They're just a few of the many to choose from, but they are ones that we believe can serve to strengthen your family collectively and as individuals.

FAITH. Going to church together as a family, having family devotions, praying together before meals and at bedtime, and your children seeing you having your own quiet time are all powerful ways to help your children value faith.

FAMILY TIME. Go on walks as a family. Ride bikes. Read books out loud at dinner or at bedtime. Play games. Watch a favorite family show. Eat dinner together. Children who have strong relationships with their parents are more likely to learn from and own their family values.

SERVING. Sponsor a family at Christmas. Rake leaves for an elderly neighbor. Take a sick friend a meal. Go on a mission trip. Build a habitat house. Do something special for your child. Help kids come up with an idea to surprise and serve a sibling. One of the best builders in self-esteem in children is to give them opportunities to see that they can make a difference.

RELATIONSHIPS. Make your home a kid-friendly place, whatever age your kids are. Invite their friends over. Let them have sleepovers. Lead a Bible study for guys or girls their age. Let them see you spend time with your own friends. As your children get older, one of the ways you value them is to value their friends. It also gives you the inside scoop on what is going on in their peer group.

HONESTY/INTEGRITY. I know many parents who give consequences but lessen those consequences, if their child tells the truth. This reinforces the value of honesty. Tell them you're proud of them when they make hard choices that reflect their integrity.

RESPECT. Every home should have a bottom-line level of respect. You can have words that are not acceptable and come with an immediate consequence such as *stupid*, *fat*, or *hate*. Have your children write apology letters if they hurt each other.

GOOD MANNERS. Make thank-you notes a requirement. Make sure your kids know how to act when talking on a phone, rather than just texting. Have table manners challenges at dinner. Go out to eat at nice restaurants for opportunities to practice. Teach them to speak to other people, even if you have to wait in discomfort until they do.

HEALTHY EATING. Teach your children healthy eating when they are young. Have healthy choices at home, but don't make food such an issue that it takes on too much power. Eating disorders are increasingly prevalent in kids, and too much restriction can cause a child to rebel even in his food choices.

GRATITUDE. Practice gratitude as a family, from when your children are young. Take time, not just on Thanksgiving, to go around the table to say what you're each thankful for. Have a thankfulness journal. Make gratitude a priority, individually and together.

KINDNESS. Give your children opportunities to show kindness. Let them pick out a treat at the store for a sibling. Point out when you see them showing kindness to a classmate or friend. Let them be a part of birthday and Christmas gifts. Kindness will be more natural for your children than your adolescents, so start reinforcing this one early. And then watch carefully for any chance to catch and encourage your child for being kind.

Consistent Responsibilities

Giving your child responsibilities is a tough one. It comes with a million questions for most parents. What are they capable of? What is fair? Do you make it a requirement for being a part of the family, or do you pay them for their chores? Is it part of their allowance? Do you make a chart? How do you make a chart? What do you do if they don't do their chores? Are responsibilities really that big a deal?

When I started working at Daystar, I joined the staff of our summer camp, Camp Hopetown. There were a few things that summer that took me by surprise. The first was the way the camp was taken care of. The kids did it. They cleaned and watered plants. They even cooked the meals, including a full-out Thanksgiving dinner. I remember hearing this and expecting the kids to dread cleanup. I thought they would cringe the day their turn to cook rolled around and that they would be happy when it was over. Instead, the kids volunteered for extra meals. They sang and danced during cleanup. That was the second thing that surprised me. They actually *enjoyed* having responsibilities at camp. The chores made them feel important and showed them that we believed they were capable.

In your house, your children may not sing and dance when they're asked to do chores. They may not volunteer to help you cook dinner. But we believe that responsibilities are a big deal. We believe doing their part in consistently contributing not only helps children of all ages learn responsibility but also helps them feel important.

What responsibilities do your children have at home?

What system do you have for encouraging and implementing those responsibilities?

Toddlers and Responsibilities

You did not read that heading wrong. Toddlers are capable of responsibilities. When they're old enough to walk, they're old enough to learn to clean up after themselves . . . at least a little.

START AS LITTLE AS THEY ARE. The attention span of a toddler is not long. Toddlers also aren't great multitaskers. So as you give them instructions, give them one at a time: Put your shoes in the closet. Take your clothes to the basket. Keep it simple and clear and they'll be more likely to follow your instructions.

GROW THEIR CHORES WITH THEM. As your toddler gets older, the chores can become more complicated, although still not very. It can move from "Pick up one toy at a time," to "Pick up your toys."

SUPERVISE. Your little one is not a self-starter. He will forget what he's supposed to do as soon as you leave the room. Stay with him to remind them.

MAKE A ROUTINE. Picking their toys up before bed every night makes it easier to remember. Toddlers learn to tie the time to the action.

MAKE IT FUN. When possible, make a game or a challenge out of cleaning up. Timed challenges can be especially exciting for boys, and girls love dramatic ones with a little backstory added in. "The fairies are coming to clean your room, but they need your help. Your shoes are too heavy for them to carry . . ." If you have several children who argue about the "fairness" of jobs, have them work as a team, with each having an individual task.

ENCOURAGE OFTEN. Little ones need lots of positive attention. As we've said repeatedly, they want to please you. And they'll be more likely to want to do their chores again when they see how happy it makes you.

LET THEM HELP. Toddlers not only want to please you; they want to be like you. Give your son a little broom and let him follow along behind you. Give your daughter a dust rag. Let your kids help you with meals. It makes them feel they're helping you and being like you at the same time.

WATCH YOUR EXPECTATIONS. With toddlers, so much of teaching responsibilities is just that—teaching. They will forget a lot. Remember that they're just learning. You can put them in time-out (or another consequence) if they deliberately defy you and go the other direction. But otherwise, remember you're teaching a pattern of responsibility, just as you're trying to establish a pattern of consistency.

AND OF COURSE, BE CONSISTENT. If you only have them pick up their shoes sometimes, they're much less likely to remember than if they always take their shoes to the closet. Repetition makes things stick.

Let's talk about some specifics. What are toddlers capable of? What can you expect? These are a few examples of responsibilities for toddlers:

- Picking up after themselves
- Placing their clothes in a hamper
- Putting their shoes in the closet
- Putting away their toys
- Taking their plate to the sink—for older toddlers
- Dusting or cleaning with you

Toddlers can help. In fact, toddlers really want to. Give them regular opportunities to learn responsibility now and you will set the stage for greater responsibility later.

Children and Responsibilities

I was a bed-maker growing up. I just naturally liked my bed made, so I made it every day. I picked up my room too. It's not that I was such a responsible child. I think I was really just developing some OCD habits early. But besides my compulsiveness in wanting my room to be clean, I remember one other thing about my cleaning habits growing up. I wanted my mom to be proud. I wanted her to walk in my room and say, "Sissy, you've done a great job!"

Your child wants the same thing. He wants to hear your praise of his behavior. He wants you to be pleased with and proud of him. Much of his learning responsibility in these years has to do with the payoff . . . whether it's stickers on a chart, a reward, allowance, or just your praise. Actually, we should say "*and* your praise," because whether it is accompanied by stickers or dollars, praise will always be the most important part of his payoff. And whatever system you choose, consistency is the key ingredient.

SHOW YOUR PRIDE. Tell her when she's been responsible. Whether you're checking off a chart or handing her money, tell her how proud you are of her and why.

MAKE HIM FEEL THAT YOU KNOW HE'S RESPONSIBLE. Your child will rise to your level of belief in him. Give him opportunities to do things for himself. Give him ways he can contribute. In these years, you have more impact on your child's self-esteem than anyone else. He will believe what you do about him. Give him opportunities to prove himself to you and him both.

MAKE CHORES A PART OF NORMAL FAMILY LIFE.
Whether it's taking out the trash or setting the table, give him
regular responsibilities. Helping around the house can help him
see that he has something to contribute and can ward off some
of the entitlement that is so rampant among kids today.

GIVE AN ALLOWANCE. Have a set amount of money
that you give your children every week. Let the money increase
as they get older. With that money, they can learn to save and
give. You can even make jars that say things like "Give," "Save,"
and "Live," teaching kids to save and tithe their money, with a
little play money left over. It's empowering for a child to have
a chance to choose where he spends his money. We also know
children who get to choose which charity they'll donate their
"give" money to. Some of our favorite gifts at Daystar are the
$10.47 gifts we get from elementary school students. If your kids
give, let them take the money to the organization and hand it to
a person. That way, they can see the impact on a person's face,
knowing they made a difference.

LET THEM EARN EXTRA MONEY WITH EXTRA
WORK. We know several little entrepreneurs who wash cars,
clean bathrooms, and pull weeds to help save for the iPod Touch
or big-ticket item they're wanting. Give your children the chance
to earn money and experience the satisfaction of buying something they've worked for.

GIVE THEM SOMETHING TO CARE FOR. If you've
ever met us, heard us speak, or been to Daystar, you know we
are dog people. We believe in the power of pets, especially in
the lives of children. Caring for a pet can be a huge source of
comfort for a child and a teacher of responsibility. Start small,
literally, with a goldfish or hamster, and let your kids work their

way toward a larger pet as they show responsibility. Let them walk the dog; even if they're smaller, they can walk with you and hold the leash. Try to enlist them to feed and water your pets and clean out their bowls and cages. We say "try" here, because we know *many* families who've bought pets for children who *promise* they'll care for their pets . . . only to forget or become too busy. We're going for patterns, remember? And we know one family who gave the child's dog away because she wasn't fulfilling her promise. Kids won't fulfill all of their promises. Keep realistic expectations and know you are teaching them responsibility and much more when you give them something to care for.

MATCH RESPONSIBILITIES TO AGE LEVEL. Your child won't know how to clean a toilet until you show him. He won't know how to vacuum or how much to feed the dog. Remember to always teach first and start with smaller tasks. Be patient in the process. Then, as your children get older, they become more capable of bigger contributions.

DON'T BE IN SO MUCH OF A HURRY THAT YOU DON'T LET THEM HELP. I mentioned earlier how the kids cook the meals at camp. It is actually one counselor and typically three or four kids who cook the meals . . . at least it usually is. One year, we had a counselor who would fix breakfast before the kids woke up. She "didn't want the toast to be burned or for it to take too long." Cooking with little ones can make for a few burned edges. But the point is that they feel a sense of accomplishment when they help. It may slow you down in the process, but a little burned toast is worth the confidence it builds in your child.

MAKE RESPONSIBILITY A FAMILY PROJECT. Wash the car together and give each family member a certain job. Grow a garden where everyone pitches in. Build a swing set. Join forces to make something happen that they, and you, can be proud of together.

CREATE A CHORE CHART. Trying to remember three chores can feel like memorizing Shakespeare for your elementary student. Kids just can't do it with all of the other things that are on their minds. Visuals can help. Create a chart. Charts serve as great reminders and provide kids with a sense of accomplishment as they put checks or stickers on completed tasks. We talk about chore charts a lot with parents. The most common question is, "So how do I make one?" We found this summary online, which we thought would be a helpful guideline.

How to Make Your Own Chore Chart[8]

- Draw a large grid with 8 columns and approximately 10 rows on poster-sized paper or cardboard.
- Use bright colors and designs to make the chart attractive.
- Label the first column "chores," and the remaining columns according to the days of the week.
- In the first column, paste cutout pictures or stickers that represent different chores (i.e. a goldfish for feeding fish or a toothbrush for brushing teeth).
- Together with your child, place a sticker in the appropriate square each time s/he completes a chore.
- Be sure to congratulate your child enthusiastically and celebrate when placing the stickers on the chart.

The chart will change as your child gets older. There is also a lot of flexibility in the art of chart making. You can substitute words for pictures. You can add characteristics you want your child to work on, such as kindness or gratitude, and place a sticker or a check mark when you see him display those qualities. You can also tie rewards to the chart, such as a small reward for five checks in a week, a bigger reward for ten, and so on.

Repeatedly in this section, we've said phrases like "Give him the chance to contribute," and "Let her feel a sense of accomplishment." Responsibility is empowering in the life of a child. It builds his confidence in who he is and what he is capable of. But it requires you to be consistent in what you require of him. Give your children this opportunity. There will be enough coming at them that will shake their confidence in these years and the years to come. Arm them with a sense of responsibility that causes them to believe in themselves. And then you will have a chance to show and say how very much you believe in them too.

Teenagers and Responsibilities

Molly was just asked to come to Washington, D.C., to be commended for the hours she's invested and dollars she's raised for her two favorite charities, one of which happens to be Daystar. Molly is in eighth grade and knows that she makes a difference. Molly is one of the many capable teenagers we see at Daystar. In fact, they all are. And whether they admit it or not, they're all hungry to see their lives have impact. They want to be responsible. They want your respect, and if they're making good choices, they feel that they deserve it.

I have met several parents over the years who say, "They're just teenagers." These parents are typically trying to excuse some irresponsible behavior their children have just committed.

They are not "just teenagers." They're fledgling adults who need to learn the tools that will propel them safely and responsibly into the real world. It's your job, in their teenage years, to equip them with these tools. And we believe consistently applying these principles will help you do so.

RESPONSIBILITY IS CAUGHT. In a section called "Responsibility Is Caught, not Taught" in *Parenting Teens with Love and Logic*, the authors said "Responsibility isn't something that a parent passes on to a teen by lectures, threats, or intimidation. Instead responsibility and the self-esteem that goes along with it are passed on through covert messages that allow teens to build their character on their strengths. We must give teens opportunities to make decisions, as well as mistakes."[9] Give your teens the opportunity to catch responsibility.

GIVE THEM FLEXIBLE BOUNDARIES. I meet with many parents of teenagers highly frustrated with the state of their kids' rooms. "The piles are literally up to my knees," they'll say. "I find dishes and glasses from weeks ago. Does choosing my battles mean I need to let go of their rooms? It's my house, after all." It *is* your house. And a clean room may be a battle you choose to fight. If so, give them that boundary, but be flexible in it. "Clean your room now," can be a difficult task for a high school student who goes from school to cheerleading practice and then has three hours of homework. What we've found to be much more effective is a regular, once-a-week cleanup, potentially tied to an activity the teen wants to do. For example, "You can go out on Friday night as soon as your room is clean."

LET THE CONSEQUENCES DO THE TEACHING. If her room is then not clean, she can't go out on Friday night. We have teenagers who schedule and then forget their own counseling appointments. Their parents don't ground them, but they make them pay half or the full fee for the missed appointment. Let them live with the natural consequences of their irresponsibility.

REQUIRE SOMETHING OF THEM. Melissa is amazing with teenage boys. I have watched countless boys over the years who come to Hopetown angry and hardened but leave camp tender and responsive to God's Spirit. It's partly because she's such a gifted Bible teacher and partly because she needs them . . . or makes them feel that way. Melissa gives them opportunities to work on her Jeep or lay sod. They walk away feeling that they've helped and made a difference, rather than just "been teenagers." Require something of them. Have them help around the house and continue doing chores.

GIVE THEM A VOICE. When you're handing out chores for the family, let your teenagers pick first. The younger kids will feel that it's a privilege, and your adolescents will feel more respected. If you want to volunteer somewhere as a family, let your teenagers choose where. Teenagers often lose their voice through adolescence and are afraid to stand out. Give them a chance to use their voices in a way that truly can make a difference.

REQUIRE RESPONSIBILITY OUTSIDE THE HOME. In our *Modern Parents, Vintage Values* parenting seminar, David talks about how every boy should have a job at some point during adolescence. Every teen needs some place outside of the home to prove his or her responsibility. It can be a regular job, babysitting, serving as an officer in a club, or even a weekly volunteer opportunity. Let your child choose the place, but you can require his consistent participation. Working and serving in this way will increase both his responsibility and his confidence.

INCREASE THE RESPONSIBILITIES WITH AGE. Your seventeen-year-old can do her own laundry. In reality, she needs to learn, as she'll have to do it herself in a year. As they get older, teenagers need to learn to be responsible with their calendars, their finances, and themselves. Be strategic in adding to their responsibilities as they move through adolescence.

REWARD THEIR RESPONSIBILITY. As teenagers get older, their privileges should increase with each year . . . as long as they've earned them. Your seventeen-year-old should not have the same bedtime as your fourteen-year-old, if she is acting responsibly. If your son is making good choices, he is proving himself to be trustworthy. Give him more of your trust. As we've said before, kids rise to the level of belief you place in them. They want opportunities to prove their responsibility.

Consistency continues to be vital in teaching teenagers responsibility. If you only require him to keep his room clean sometimes, he'll never remember. If she volunteers somewhere once a year, she doesn't truly have the opportunity to see that she makes a difference. Give them choices and opportunities. Require of them, but with flexibility. They need chances to catch the responsibility that teenagers are capable of.

Consistent Discipline

When we speak to parents across the country, the subject we are asked about the most is discipline. It holds true for every age. Parents of toddlers ask about bedtime and tantrums. Parents of elementary students have questions about whining and all-out disobedience. And parents of teens wonder about disrespect: How much is too much?

We'd love to answer all of those questions and more in this chapter. But it would require an entire book. In fact, we've already discovered books that address those issues beautifully: the Love and Logic series. We'll defer to them on the specifics. But what we want to do is equip you with principles for discipline. We believe if you use these ideas with consistency, discipline will be less of an issue in your home and you'll be freed up to better enjoy life as a family. But remember, consistency is the key.

Toddlers and Discipline

TEACHING COMES FIRST. Toddlers don't automatically know what will elicit a "no" from you. Be realistic in your expectations. They don't know not to crawl down the stairs or put their faces in a dog's face. You have to teach them.

USE SIMPLE, REPETITIVE STATEMENTS . . . AGAIN. Just like before, the repetition will help them learn. "Uh oh,"[10] is the authors' favorite sentence in *Love and Logic Magic for Early Childhood*. This statement signals that the child is heading toward a "no-no." *No-no* works too, by the way. Toddlers need a simple statement that is an indicator to stop.

CHANGE THEIR LOCATION. Accompany your statement with physically picking them up and moving them to another spot. You can distract them with something else when they get there.

REMOVE THE OFFENDING OBJECT. If your son has hit your dog with a toy, take away the toy as you repeat your statement. If he starts to throw his food, remove his meal. Taking the object that is causing trouble helps ensure that he doesn't repeat the offense. It proves that you're in charge.

TIME-OUT. Toddlers are old enough to be sent to time-out. You can send them to their rooms "until they can come out and speak kindly." If they're small and you're worried about them, you can sit outside the door during their imprisonment. You can also select a special chair in a quiet room that can serve as time-out, as well.

HANDLING TANTRUMS. Tantrums can be difficult with toddlers and small children because they often happen in public, but what your children are really wanting is your attention. One option is not to give them any. Keep walking. They'll eventually catch up. Or you can make it a game. "Your last tantrum was much more impressive than this one. Keep working on it, and I know you'll get there." It may sound sarcastic, but it takes the power out of the emotion they're trying to use to manipulate you. If your child is particularly struggling with this one, you can reward her for good behavior after a given period of time. For example, "You were so kind in the grocery store today that you get to pick out one treat before we go home." Whether you use positive or negative reinforcement, the most important idea is not to give in to tantrums, as it will only serve to strengthen the behavior.

DON'T LET WHINING WORK. Toddlers learn the art of whining before they even learn to speak in sentences. And they often carry it over into childhood . . . some even into adolescence. Don't give in. If your son or daughter is whining, just respond with, "I only listen to children who speak with real voices, not whines." And then don't listen. Consistently. Once your child learns that whining doesn't work, he'll stop.

DON'T GIVE IN TO THE BEDTIME BATTLE. Establish a routine with your child at bedtime. Be consistent. Maybe it's a bath, story, and then bed. The predictability helps him feel more secure. And don't give in to negotiations. You can give him a choice, such as, "Would you like to go to bed now or in five minutes?" or "Would you like to read a story or sing a song?" Choices help kids feel some sense of control in a time that can feel scary. Go through your routine and then leave the room. Tell your son you'll be back to check on him in ten minutes and make sure he's okay. But he needs to learn to self-soothe. Giving in to the demands of a toddler at bedtime can create habits that take years to break.

A pattern of consistency is especially important in disciplining toddlers. You are establishing the pecking order of your home. They need to know that you are in charge and that you are going to handle things in a loving, consistent manner. It helps them feel more secure and increases the bonding that takes place during these pivotal years.

Children and Discipline

How did your parents discipline you as a child? Do you handle things similarly with your own children? We see many parents today disciplining in reaction to the way they were brought up. Maybe their parents were heavy-handed, and they don't want to crush their child's spirit. We see a lot of parents who reason with their children more than discipline them. "Giving them a good talking-to" is as firm as it gets. But it's mostly just trying to make their children understand why something is wrong. Kids typically already know why it's wrong. They just want to get away with it. To use reason with a child instead of discipline gives him too much power. When you speak to children as if they're adults, they start to believe they should be treated that way in all things. And you end up with entitled kids.

Children need discipline. They need parents who are firm and consistent in their consequences. Children who are allowed to get away with being the worst versions of themselves start to believe that's who they are. When you discipline your child, you are, in effect, saying, "I believe you're capable of more."

SAY WHAT YOU MEAN AND MEAN WHAT YOU SAY. Don't throw out blanket statements such as, "You'll never see a basketball again if you don't stop throwing it against the wall." He will see a basketball again, and you look foolish and reactionary to make a statement you can't follow up on. Say what you mean. And then follow through. It's not the statement that's the teacher; it's the action. If you're a parent who doesn't follow through, your child knows. I have kids tell me often that they know how to get out of a punishment. Your children will respect you more when you make true statements that you follow through on.

BEGIN AT HOME. If you don't want your children to whine in public, don't let them whine at home. Make them use their big-kid voices. If you want them to say "please" and "thank you," have them say it to you at home. What works at home will eventually work outside the home.

GIVE THEM A CHANCE, but only one. For example, your child will often not know that he's speaking disrespectfully. You can give him a warning before you give him a consequence. A warning gives him a chance to learn self-control.

GIVE THEM A CHOICE. Your warning can be a choice. "You can speak to me respectfully or spend some time in your room, calming yourself down. It's your choice." That way, they feel some degree of control. You're also communicating that the consequences are due to their poor choice, rather than your "strict" parenting. Or, when their rooms continue to be a mess,

"You can use the clothes [or toys, etc.] you clean up. I'll keep the others until I know you will take good care of them." They have a choice, but you are ultimately in control.

LOVE THEM TOO MUCH TO ARGUE. This is another one from our friends Cline and Fay. It's one of those statements that will free you and often infuriate them. Don't argue. They're arguing either to manipulate you or vent their emotions. Neither is helpful. Tell them, "I love you too much to argue,"[11] and walk away. It works great with teens too.

PROVIDE CONSISTENT BOUNDARIES. "The car leaves at 7:00 a.m. for school," for example. If your child is late, he has to wait until you get home from taking his siblings, and then maybe even running a few errands. And then he likely gets a tardy. If you're a working parent, maybe he has to wait at home or even go to work with you and sit bored until you have a break to drive him to school. Another example can be, "There is no fighting in the car. The cost, when you do, is $5.00. You can pay me with cash, chores, or toys." Children need to know what is expected of them. "If you borrow your sister's clothes without asking, you will pay her rent, $1.00 a day for each piece of clothing." If you consistently maintain boundaries, they may push in the beginning but will eventually realize that the boundaries are not moving.

TURN MISTAKES INTO LEARNING OPPORTUNITIES. If your child makes a mistake, ask questions about how she'd like to handle the situation. Give her opportunities to think for herself and make choices. Kids feel better about themselves when they come up with the solution. If they're struggling, ask if they'd like help. Your child needs to learn problem-solving skills, and it's not too early to start.

PARENT OUT OF EMPATHY, NOT EMOTIONAL REACTIONS. Things can become heated quickly in any discipline issue. Emotional reactions, such as anger or guilt-inducing drama, don't help. They make your child feel too much power, knowing he can cause such a strong reaction in you. He often feels like he's a bad child, rather than a child who is behaving badly. When you offer a choice with a consequence tied to it, you can be empathetic when the consequences come. "I know it's really hard to have to pull a card at school," or "We'll really miss you at the movie tonight" are empathetic responses. Empathy maintains the relationship. And it's the consequence, not your emotion, that teaches the lesson. The emotions just confuse the issue and your child.

KNOW WHEN TO WALK AWAY. When your anger is stronger than the situation warrants, you may need to walk away. If you're in the car, you may need to stop talking. Wait to handle the situation once you get home and have calmed down. Negative emotions don't reinforce positive behavior. You may have to give yourself time to discipline objectively.

USE CHARTS AS A SYSTEM OF REWARDS. You can use the same type of chart you used with your toddlers, but with school-age responsibilities and tasks. You can use it to reward the positive side of his negative behavior. For example, if your son is treating his sister poorly, "Being kind to your sister" can be on the chart. If your daughter is struggling with lying, honesty could be on the list. Point out the positive behaviors in your school-age children, not just the negatives.

"Just what are helpful consequences, anyway?" you may be asking. We'll list a few that we've found useful over the years with school-age children.

- Chores, such as cleaning a bathroom, picking up s[...]
  in the yard, etc.
- Running laps around the house, adding laps the longer
  the behavior goes on
- Time-out in the child's bedroom
- Writing an apology letter to the person offended
- Making logical restitution, such as paying for a broken
  window
- Taking away technology time—with whatever gadgets
  matter to your child, such as television, iPods, cell
  phones, etc.
- Adjusting bedtime with each infraction—five minutes
  earlier, etc.
- Keeping them home from an activity they want to
  participate in, such as going to a friend's house.

You may have noticed that we haven't mentioned spanking. There are lots of opinions on the great spanking debate. What works for one child may not work for another. Swatting a child's hand is different from hitting her bottom with a spoon, as many parents of our generation did. As a counselor, I hear kids tell me how they secretly feel about a whole host of discipline issues, including spanking. What most of them say is that spanking is easy because it's over so quickly. I tend to believe there are other options, and options that stimulate more thinking on the part of your child.

Whatever you choose in terms of discipline, stick with the plan. If you're a parent who changes discipline strategies with the seasons, your child will know. He'll just wait it out until this particular stage passes. It's the repetition that reinforces your message. Again, consistency is vital, with children of any age.

Teenagers and Discipline

"If I disciplined her every time she did something wrong, she'd be in trouble all the time." We've heard this statement from many parents of teenagers over the years, and it's often accompanied by much frustration and worry. The stakes get higher for your adolescents. Trouble for a school-age child was getting caught lying about his homework or staying up too late on a school night. For a teenager, trouble has greater risks, especially today. Teens are surrounded by kids who are making poor choices by sneaking out, posting inappropriate pictures of themselves online, sexting, drinking, using life-threatening drugs. It's a scary world . . . and one that your teenagers are exposed to on a daily basis.

So, what can you do? How do you protect them and allow them to begin to enter the world of adulthood? What battles do you choose and what consequences do you give? And how in the world do you do it consistently?

BE THE PARENT. If you're a consistent parent who disciplines your teen, she will get angry with you. This can be hard. You may be tempted to give in, wanting her to like you. But it is more important in these years that she respects you than likes you. Be the parent. Give teens consequences. Just as in their younger years, if they are allowed to be the worst versions of themselves, that is who they'll believe they are. Hold them to a higher standard.

LEAVE THE DRAMA TO THEM. Emotions can escalate more quickly between teenagers and their parents than any other combination of ages. Save your emotions for your spouse, your friends, or your counselor. Your adolescents will hurt you. Part of the purpose of adolescence is for them to pull away and become independent. This, in itself, is painful on the best days. When they are angry and disrespectful, you'll want to act just like them. Be the adult. Process your feelings with other adults who can handle them. Teens need you to be stronger than they are in order to feel safe and secure. When you react dramatically, they feel either as strong or stronger than you.

CHOOSE YOUR BATTLES. You've heard it a million times, and for good reason. You can, like the parent we quoted earlier, end up in a constant battle with your teen if you don't. Too much discipline can cause teens to lose hope.

LET THE CONSEQUENCES FIT THE CRIME. In other words, give smaller consequences for smaller infractions. For example, take away your daughter's cell phone for a day for disrespect. Take away everything for a month for sneaking out. And if there are natural consequences that occur, such as a school suspension or being penalized on a sports team, don't rescue your teen. Let someone else be the bad guy for a change, and let your teenager learn from the natural consequences imposed on him.

ASSUME THE BEST. When your child makes a mistake, don't assume it was a vengeful act against you. The brains of teenagers aren't finished developing. They make bad choices. To assume the best can take the emotion out of the situation and help you see things objectively.

FOCUS ON THE PRESENT, NOT THE PAST. I talk to teenagers every day who feel that they can't earn trust back with their parents. They've made one big mistake in the past, and it comes up every time they make a little one. There may be times when your teenager causes you to lose trust in her. Talk about that, but give her opportunities to earn trust back, without holding her past mistakes over her.

GIVE THEM HOPE. I am an advocate of short-term, intense consequences for teens. When they're grounded for six months, they don't even remember why they were grounded in the first place. Let them know the consequences aren't forever. Give them an end point. If they've violated your trust, let them know specifically how they can earn it back.

ALLOW THEM TO MAKE MISTAKES. If you don't give your children privileges, they'll never make mistakes. Let the rope out gradually as they get older so they experience more and more of the freedom that will be theirs when they hit eighteen. They'll make mistakes, and then you can pull the rope right back in. But they learn from their mistakes and the consequences that follow. If you don't give them some degree of freedom, they won't have an opportunity to make mistakes.

PROTECT THE GOOD THINGS. Don't ground your children from things that build their character. We have kids who are grounded from counseling groups at Daystar. I know children who are grounded from their small groups at church. Don't take away the very voices that support your decisions and encourage your teens to make good choices.

DON'T LOSE SIGHT OF WHO THEY CAN BE. When your teenagers fail, they will feel like failures. Even as you discipline them, they need you to remember who they can be. Continue to believe in and encourage them when they make mistakes. Most teenagers don't believe in themselves. In those times, your version of who they are may be the best there is to offer.

What kinds of consequences work with teenagers? We believe that the removal of what matters the most has the greatest power. What does your child like to do with his or her free time? In today's world, it often has to do with technology. Cell phones, computers, and gaming systems pack a lot of punch in terms of consequences. Social events do as well. You can also give teens chores to help out around the house. Don't feel pressure to hand out consequences immediately. You can tell them you'll get back to them, which gives them time to worry and gives you time to do some research. Logical consequences work well too. If your son is thirty minutes late for curfew, have him come in thirty minutes early the next weekend. It can even be beneficial to have teenagers help set their own consequences. I do that regularly with families in counseling. What do they believe is a fair punishment for the crime? You may be surprised at what they come up with.

Teenagers are so inconsistent within themselves that they crave consistency in their parents. They're so emotional that they need you to be a stable, steady, kind yet firm presence in their lives. They need you to be the parent. They need you to teach them about the world and what it means to be a responsible adult.

As you have read this chapter, what have you noticed about the ways you discipline your children?

How would you like to discipline differently?

In what areas can you be more consistent as a parent?

What are three specific ways you could start being more consistent today?

Walter Wangerin says, "Discipline is an extended and carefully managed event, not a sudden, spontaneous, personal

reaction to the child's behavior."[12] Don't give in to spontaneous, personal reactions, no matter how old your child is. Be
consistent. Be consistent in the ways you teach her values. Be
consistent in the responsibilities that you require in your family.
And be consistent in your discipline. Consistency creates security in children of all ages. It strengthens your relationship and
builds a connection and trust with your child that we believe
will last a lifetime.

6.

Being a Playful Parent

—with Melissa

DECEMBER 1906. NEW YORK NEEDED *PETER PAN*. The play came at one of those discouraged moments when the public mind was occupied to an almost morbid degree with huge and vexing problems, and with things that were going wrong. Legalized evil-doing was rampant in business and politics, the exposure of fraud was the principal business of those who were not committing it. Cynicism was the dominant note In literature and dramatic art, a cheerful, clever, twentieth-century cynicism, but a bitter and depressing influence, for all that. At such a moment came Peter Pan, created in the mind of a man of insight and gentleness, embodied by a woman beautiful in life and thought, with the soul of an artist, and the heart of a child. . . . Playing Peter

Pan is not acting a role. It is embodying a living thought. It is
expressing the life-force in the simplest, most beautiful way
by teaching us to look at life from a child's point of view. . . .
Realities that seemed formidable are found not to be real
at all, and all sorts of lovely illusions are dreams that may
come true.[1]

New York needed *Peter Pan*. In the midst of a culture of discouragement, New York needed to be encouraged to look at life from a child's point of view. That was the heart behind J. M. Barrie's work, not just to give us an example of a boy who never grew up. (Although we've certainly gleaned that too.) He intended to give us the choice to see the world through a child's eyes.

Being a grown-up parent speaks to an experience in the present that triggers pain from your past. It is not a choice in those moments to return to our past. It's an involuntary reaction caused by unresolved pain that makes us temporarily revert to childish ways. In the last chapter, we talked about putting those ways behind. In this chapter, it sounds as if we're telling you to pick them right back up.

Fast-forward from 1906 to 1991. Peter Pan has grown up. He's put his childish ways behind, but he's also lost his sense of play. He has become a weary, stressed-out, cutthroat, mergers-and-acquisitions lawyer named Peter Banning in the movie *Hook*. He is also father to two children who long for him to play. "Not right now, children," and similar statements fly effortlessly from the lips of this Peter. And it isn't until he chooses to have an imagination (and a food fight at that) that he begins to reclaim his sense of play.

Making a choice is the difference in these two chapters.

Choosing to play. Choosing to enjoy life as your five- or ten- or fourteen-year-old self. This chapter is about choosing to live with a lightheartedness that comes from seeing the world through a child's eyes.

Sissy and I recently had dinner with our dear friend Cindy and her two daughters, Olivia, who is Sissy's goddaughter, and Savannah, who is mine. As we were finishing dinner, Cindy said excitedly to her girls (who are twelve and nine respectively), "We've got to hurry up and get home so we can play hide-and-seek." I think Sissy and I must have simultaneously looked a little surprised. "We play it every night before bed," Cindy said. "We love it." And from the looks on all three of their faces, it was obvious they did.

Choosing to play. Our hope for you is that, as you read this chapter, you will be reminded of the importance of taking the time to play hide-and-seek, to laugh, and to choose to go back to those times of lighthearted love for whatever you're doing in the moment.

Obstacles to Play

The words written about New York in 1906 could just as easily be written about Nashville or Little Rock, Dallas or Birmingham, or whatever city you live in today. We have become, in many ways, the stressed-out, gray-faced adults Anne Lamott mentioned in chapter 3.

I heard once that work, rest, and play should all be balanced in equal measure in our lives. LOL on that one. We don't slow down enough to even type out full words in our texts. How are you in the balance? I would guess work takes up a majority of your time and your energy, whether it's work at an office or work at home. Culturally, we do not rest or play well.

One summer, I taught on that idea to our staff. We talked about committing as a camp to giving our campers ample opportunity to rest, to work by helping out and giving to others, and to play. I remember, later that summer, a box of water guns and toys arrived from our board of directors. One staff member spontaneously pulled out the first water gun, and it was all over. We ended up in a thirty-minute water fight, guys versus girls, all over the house and yard. And I, as a fifty-something-year-old, was right there in the midst of them.

The main reason that day is so vivid in my mind is because it was only one day. If we had spontaneous water fights every summer, they would all blend together. But, typically, I'm too worried about the water getting all over the house. I'm thinking about what I'm going to teach in our next devotional time. I'm focused on planning and preparing and cleaning up.

We all have obstacles that keep us from a sense of play. We get out of balance and lean too hard on the work side, until we have no option but to rest. Play gets lost somewhere in the mix. I want to look at just a few of our obstacles, and our fears that hide underneath.

I'LL LOOK SILLY. I'm trying to come off as a put-together, competent, confident adult. If I try line dancing, I'll look silly because I don't have any rhythm. I don't want people to see that I'm not all I pretend to be.

I'M NOT ACCOMPLISHING ANYTHING. I have too much to do and don't have time to be unproductive. It feels ir-responsible when there are so many things I need to take care of.

I'M TOO TIRED. I got up early and have worked hard all day. I just want to sit and watch TV.

I DON'T WANT TO DRAW ATTENTION TO MYSELF. I've gained weight, and I don't want everyone looking at me when it's my turn to kick the ball.

I'M AFRAID. I don't want to play Taboo because I don't want anyone to be critical or judgmental. I just can't think that fast, and I don't want someone to yell at me or be disappointed that I let our team down.

I CAN'T DO THAT LIKE I USED TO. I used to be a good skier, but now I can't really remember how. I just get so tense and tight trying to do it like I did back then that it wouldn't be fun for anybody.

WHAT WOULD THE OTHER PARENTS THINK? I don't see any other parents spending time playing with their kids. They might think I'm irresponsible.

I DON'T KNOW WHAT TO DO. My kids want me to come outside and play with them, but I don't know what I'm supposed to do. I'm just not like that. I'd rather cheer them on and watch them have fun.

MY KIDS DON'T WANT ME TO PLAY WITH THEM. They don't really want me around. They just want me to do things for them and have things ready so they can play.

One in five parents say they've forgotten how to play. One in three say play is boring.[2]

How do you feel about play?

Which or how many of these obstacles have you caught yourself saying recently?

How often do you sit on the floor and play games with your child? Do you join your kids in their summertime frolics around the sprinkler?

When is the last time you really laughed with your children? Or laughed without them?

Dan Allender, a friend and mentor as well as a psychologist and author, says that our culture regards play as a "guilty pastime." "We live in a self-absorbed, narcissistic age, but it's still an age of work, not play . . . busyness, not recreation: and productivity, not Sabbath."[3]

It is time for us to change our perspective on play. Your children need you to play, and you need to for yourself. Play is productive. It loosens the tension that is all too familiar as a parent and frees your soul to experience joy.

The Purpose of Play

Dr. Stuart Brown said:

The opposite of play is not work—the opposite of play is depression. Respecting our biologically programmed need for play can transform work. It can bring back excitement and newness to our job. Play helps us deal with difficulties, provides a sense of expansiveness, promotes mastery of our craft, and is an essential part of the creative process. Most important, true play that comes from our own inner needs and desires is the only path to finding lasting joy and satisfaction in our work. In the long run, work does not work without play.[4]

Playing with Your Kids

I remember when my dog, Blueberry, was a puppy. Sadly, Sissy, David, and I all lost beloved, older dogs over a time period of about a year. So within the course of a few months, we all three, along with Sissy's sister and mother, had puppies. That meant five puppies were romping (and pee-peeing) in and out of Hopetown and the Daystar office. We basically had our own litter of Daystar dogs. And, boy, did that litter love to play.

I learned a lot from watching the puppies play—just as they were learning a lot from each other. They learned about sharing, and when not to share (like when Sissy's dog, Lucy, came around). They learned when a playful nip didn't feel so playful to another dog (like to Sissy's dog, Lucy). They learned the pecking order of our little herd (can you already tell who was the boss?) and learned how important a nap was after a time of serious play. Play had purpose for Blueberry, Owen, Lolly, Gussy, and Lucy. It was an expression of their joy and an acknowledgment of the relationships they shared.

Play also has purpose for you and your kids. When we speak to parents, we talk about the need for every child to feel enjoyed by his or her parents. Every child needs time with his or her mom and dad that is not spent instructing, coaching, teaching, or even exhorting . . . just plain play together. It helps build a child's confidence and increases the bond between you.

As a side note, we're not only talking about watching your children play, although that's important too. Kids want an audience, and it's easy to think (especially after a hard day's work) that by watching them play, you are entering in. You can watch them play tennis and dive off diving boards, but they also want you to jump in and get a little wet right alongside them.

At camp, the kids will beg the adult counselors to get in the lake with them. I cannot even begin to count the number of kids who have said to me, "My mom won't swim with us. She doesn't like to get her hair wet." Or, "My dad comes to the lake with us, but he spends a lot of time on his phone because it's hard for him to get away from work."

Dive in. Get your hair wet. Get on the floor and play a board game. Laugh. Enjoy your children by playing with them. And then save a little time to play without them as well.

Playing for You

Several years ago, I met with a mom of two teenage girls. As we talked, she told me how frustrated her daughters were with their father's lack of time at home, from their perception. "They get so mad because he plays golf every Saturday. They think he should be at the house, helping and spending time with me. What they don't understand is how much it helps me when he does go play golf. He is a better father and husband when he comes home. It's almost like playing golf gives him the chance to let go of whatever he's worried about at work and frees him to be more present with us." And then, she added with a whisper, "I like him better when he's been playing." If we were to ask him, we would guess that he likes himself better too.

Do you remember what it was like when you were younger? School was over, your carpool dropped you off, and the first thing you wanted to do was go outside and play. You dropped your books in the kitchen as fast as you could and ran outside to grab your bike, play on your swing set, or kick a soccer ball. Play was an instinctual response to the stress of your day. You played hard until your mom called you in for supper, or for homework, and you came back inside a much freer and fuller person.

Even though our instincts today may tell us differently, play opens us up. It gives us space and time—space to process all that's going on inside of us and time to let go of our stress and tension. It helps us breathe and gives us perspective. It frees us to be more creative, more alive, and more present. It gives us a needed break from the busyness and muchness of our lives and allows us to return home more of who we are than when we left to play.

In *Surprised by Laughter*, Terry Lindvall said:

Fun finds its natural province in the activity of play, and people play at a variety of things: walking, talking, sports, tag, tickling, hide-and-go-seek, reading, writing, chasing, climbing, eating, drinking, dancing, singing, and rolling down a grassy hill. It is in play and fun that we find ourselves closest to our biological natures. We laugh from the rush of speed and wind in our faces; we laugh from splashing into cold, bracing water; we laugh in hugging and being hugged. The laughter of fun emanates from our being creatures of the earth—being physical, being creatures sensitive to touch and taste and sound and smell and sight, and being able to breathe and bounce in this adventure of life. Play allows us to be eternally young, to be like children even when we are old and wrinkly.[5]

In Matthew 18:3, Jesus tells us to be like little children. Play is one of the most direct routes to get there.

How can you bring back a sense of play to your life?

*What can you do for yourself that would be the equivalent of
throwing down your schoolbooks and hopping on your bike?*

How could you play more with your children?

Being a playful parent starts with being a playful person.
One flows freely into the other. Be like a child. Take time to play.
And allow God to refresh in you all that it takes to be a playful
parent.

Playful Parents Are . . .

FUN. Not that you have to be fun, because that can feel like
pressure. But playful parents are open to fun, when it presents
itself. And they give it plenty of opportunity to present itself.
They make time for it, allow space for it, and understand its
importance enough to give energy to it.

SPONTANEOUS. My second-grade nephew, Ben, recently
came to visit Hopetown with his dad and my mother, who is his
eighty-six-year-old great-grandmother. Because Ben is coming
to camp here for the first time this summer, I wanted him to
feel like he knew the lay of the land. So I showed him around,
pointing out the basketball goal, the rope swing, and all manner of other fun things to occupy him if he got bored. Thirty
minutes later, Ben came running up the hill to me, excitedly
shouting, "Aunt Melissa, I need a pen and some paper." Rather
than playing on any of the games or toys Hopetown houses, Ben
had spent the last half hour swinging in a hammock with my
mom. While they were swinging, they looked up at the sky and

wrote a poem, each taking a turn to write a line. He ran up to the house to get a pen to write their poem down. He had a ball simply swinging in the hammock with my mom and writing a poem. Be spontaneous. Don't feel like you have to have all of the right equipment or be in the right place to play with your kids. Use what you have—a hammock and the clouds going by, a fork and a knife to play the fork game, glasses with different levels of water and knives to make musical instruments. Make up a story as you go for a walk. Sing a song in the car. Play hide-and-seek. Some of our best moments at camp come when the boats break down and one of the interns leads us in synchronized swimming. Plan time to enjoy each other as a family also, but don't wait for the planned time. Use the moments in between to be spontaneous enough to catch the clouds going by.

LIGHTHEARTED. It can be really challenging to be lighthearted as a parent. So much about parenting creates the opposite in you. You have to be prepared. You have to be on time. You have to plan and work and organize. And then you have to worry on top of all of that—worry that your kids will be safe, that they'll be happy, that they'll get good grades and make the school play and get in the right college and marry the right person. Whew! There is so much on your mind at any given moment that it's easy for your heart to feel weighed down. I recently met a mom of two young girls, one with cancer. As I walked into the lobby, both girls were standing with their mom, wearing pink leotards, tutus, and tights. I introduced myself to the girls and then to their mom. She smiled at me and said, "Well, you can see we've been at soccer practice." The girls responded with, "*Mo-om*, we've been at ballet, not soccer." This mom had every reason in the world to have a heavy heart. But she knows the importance of play and of moments. She wants to use both to have every chance she can to connect with and enjoy her tutu-wearing girls. And more than anything else, she is a parent who is able to be lighthearted because she has a faith that enables her to be like a child, trusting in her Father.

HUMOR-FULL. Okay, we know *humor-full* is not a word, but we wanted to say *humorous* without you feeling the pressure to be funny. You don't have to have the world's wittiest sense of humor. You don't have to come up with great one-liners or tell knock-knock jokes that keep your child in stitches. Just laugh. One of our closest friends, Pace, has a wonderful laugh. She laughs freely and heartily and often, especially with her children. Her sons and daughter each think they are hilarious as a result, and they try to make her laugh even more than she already does. Scripture says, "You never saw him, yet you love him. You still don't see him, yet you trust him—with laughter and singing" (1 Peter 1:8–9 MSG). Trusting God with laughter and singing—that is a sign of a humor-full parent.

INVITING. We have all had experiences, as children and probably as adults too, when we have felt excluded from someone else's play. It was only for the "cool" kids. That kind of play is really about power more than it is the kind of play the prophet Jeremiah speaks of. Play is not exclusive. In fact, it's the opposite of being exclusive. It's inviting others to come and join in on the experience.

EXPERIENTIAL. "Taste and see that the LORD is good," says Psalm 34:8 (NIV). Play is experiential. As we mentioned before, it is easy for parents to become facilitators of fun instead of participating in the fun themselves. Join in. Experience the joy of play with your children rather than just creating it for them.

SINCERE. Goethe said, "By nothing do men show their character more than by the things they laugh at."⁶ Real play is not sarcastic. It's not cruel or flippant, although we adults can resort to that kind of play often and easily. The play we're talking about is not at the expense of anyone—including one of your children, your spouse, one of your parents, or even the funny-looking woman walking down the street. The Bible tells us that God "gives us richly all things to enjoy" (1 Tim. 6:17 NKJV). Enjoy them in the sincere, straightforward, uplifting manner that He created them for. And model that kind of play for your kids.

JOYFUL. Maybe it's not so much that playful parents start out joyful, but they have an understanding that play brings joy. Play causes joy to bubble up and out of our mouths in the form of giggles and laughter. Give it time and space to be.

Don't wait for the time to create itself. Don't wait until you're in a playful mood. Play hide-and-seek before you go to bed. Write a poem swinging in a hammock under the clouds. Get in the lake and swim. Be a playful parent. There is so much that will come against you. You will have sad days, dark days, fearful days, and even angry days. But our hope is that play will be a theme that flips and runs and skips and jumps over and in between those types of days. It is important. It has purpose beyond even that which we can see and name. God uses play in our lives, in your lives, and in the lives of your kids. He uses play to remind us of His joy. Maybe that's exactly what Henry Van Dyke was thinking when he wrote these words back in 1907, just one year after New York needed *Peter Pan*. We needed—and still need—the joy that God brings us through play.

Joyful, joyful, we adore Thee,
God of glory, Lord of love;
Hearts unfold like flow'rs before Thee,
Op'ning to the sun above.
Melt the clouds of sin and sadness;
Drive the dark of doubt away;
Giver of immortal gladness,
Fill us with the light of day!

7.

Being a Connected Parent

—with David

I HAVE A RULE THAT I NEVER RETURN E-MAILS past midnight or before 6:00 a.m. I've done it in the past, and it rarely turns out okay. I'm simply not at my best late at night or that early in the morning. I try not to make any big decisions before I've had two cups of coffee. Today I broke that rule.

Before I'd downed my first cup of coffee, I made a decision that impacted thousands of people in my life—folks I'm closely connected to. Many of them will wake this morning early to discover this life-altering decision.

I shut down my Facebook account. Facebook's slogan claims it "helps you connect and share with the people in your life." Years ago, I reluctantly gave myself to social networking at the strong urging of several friends and my last publicist. I haven't

129

regretted a decision this much since I bought a gas-guzzling, desperate-for-repairs, money-draining Ford Expedition when my children were young and we needed a car that would hold three car seats side by side.

I drank the Kool-Aid, set up an account, posted a few family photos, named my favorite albums and films, listed where I went to school and all that other junk that was designed to make me feel "connected." Following a twenty-year high school reunion, a few book signings, and random folks stumbling across my information, I collected several hundred "friends."

I never made a post in all my years as a Facebook member. I never changed my original profile photo (and was reprimanded for this frequently). I never remembered to "like" things or update my status. I never announced to the world that I was having biscuits at the Loveless Café, getting my hair cut on a Friday, recovering from the stomach virus, changing the oil in my car . . . those personal and earth-shattering events that I'd been invited to share with the universe on an hourly basis.

I'm not quite sure how the world survived without knowing that I had fish tacos for dinner last night or eggs with avocado for breakfast this morning, but somehow it kept spinning on its axis.

Now there's no information about me at all, and I am waiting to see if the sun sets tonight and rises tomorrow. I'll let you know in about an hour, because the folks at Facebook warned me that my deactivation would be effective immediately. So far, so good.

When I hit Confirm for the nineteenth time after being asked if I was sure I wanted to deactivate my account, Facebook's last-ditch effort was to choose from my hundreds of "friends" and pop their pictures up with messages that said "Derrick will miss you," and "Anne will miss you," and "Jeff will miss you."

I had to look closely at their photos because I didn't recognize Derrick or Anne. Jeff was familiar to me. I imagine they are sleeping soundly right now. I think they'll be OK today. I'm going to resist the temptation to reach out to them to see if my deactivation caused an allergic reaction.

I'm feeling confident in my decision because I don't find myself that important. I'm equally convinced that the folks at Facebook promised me something they couldn't deliver on. They promised I'd feel more "connected," but I ended up feeling more burdened and overwhelmed. I kept getting all these e-mails with counseling questions, requests from "friends," and more ways to need to communicate. "Friends" kept asking me to answer all these quizzes and to "like" their favorite things, and I couldn't keep up with the e-mails. People from high school and undergrad kept finding me and wanting to have lunch. And I kept remembering why I didn't enjoy having lunch with them then.

I will be the first to admit that a part of the promise was true. It was fun to look at the family photos of some old friends and to see evidence of parts of the world that I doubt I'll ever visit through friends' vacation photos. But the truth of the matter was that while it was enjoyable to look at Friend Keith's travels to the remote parts of the Congo, I didn't feel connected to that place. It was lovely to see the mountainous terrain and the vast oceans, but to feel connected, I need to stand in that place myself and breathe in the smell of the salt water.

In order to feel "connected" with Friend Ben, I need to be sitting across from him in a coffee shop and listening to stories about his daughter and to look at his eyes when he tells me that he's not sure he'll still have a job in a month. It doesn't work for me to read a post about Friend Cara having seen a Pulitzer Prize–winning play. I need to experience the performance to feel connected. *Real* connection takes place with *real* people through *real* experiences.

I'm old-school on so many levels. One is that I'm holding off the Facebook experience for as long as I possibly can with all three of my kids. And when I do hand over that opportunity, it will be with a number of parameters and boundaries. I'll be forced to reactivate at that point, so I can check in on how responsibly my kids are navigating Facebook. I think I'll rejoin under an alias of Julio Ragulio so that I can remain anonymous to other people but keep tabs on my kids. I'll use a photo of a famous matador for my profile photo.

One of the reasons I'll want to put parameters and boundaries around their use is that with Facebook's promise that you'll feel more connected comes the need to be on it *all* the time. How can you be connected if you aren't current?

I've heard dozens of stories from parents about what it's like for their daughters to log onto Facebook and find evidence of a party that took place that she wasn't invited to. Or for a fifteen-year-old to see the relationship status of an ex-girlfriend pictured with her new boyfriend. It feeds this need to stay "connected" at all times. It also seems to feed the need for significance. We all want to feel significant, that our lives matter.

If I post my comings and goings and blast my thoughts and ideas out to the world, it feeds some part of me that believes I'm important and significant. I'm concerned about this on so many levels for kids and adolescents. Kids already struggle with regulation. How strange that we'd invite them into an experience that supports speaking and sharing your mind and opinion on anything and everything. Rather than encouraging me to think about when and how to speak, Facebook invites me to speak about anything and everything, and to comment on what everyone else in the world feels about anything and everything. Forget the need to develop a filter.

David Elkind, a developmental theorist from the 1960s introduced two kinds of egocentrism commonly seen in adolescent development—the Imaginary Audience and the Personal Fable. The Imaginary Audience is the belief that I'm being observed and critiqued at all times. Do you see how Facebook feeds the imaginary audience phenomena, as well as adolescents' bent toward narcissism, the idea that the world revolves around them?

When you post every bowel movement, every change of clothes, where you're eating dinner, and who you're spending time with, you are being observed and critiqued by the masses. All of your "friends" are invited to comment on your comings and goings, how you look in your photographs, what they think about your music and movie choices, and anything else they care to voice an opinion about.

Danger! Danger!

One of the challenges in being a connected parent involves creating opportunities for connection, which we'll discuss in just a moment, and also modeling what real connection looks like. It's rarely surprising to me that the young men I see struggle so much in relationship. So many of them haven't developed the needed basics for relationship. They developed a false sense of connection through social media and don't have a clue what authenticity and intimacy look like. They are missing many of the nuts and bolts of relationship, like reciprocity (the give-and-take of relationship), empathy (being aware of others' feelings), or regulation (not speaking every thought that travels through my mind nor responding out of every emotion I feel). For many young men it's even difficult to make eye contact or have a normal conversation; they'd rather text or tweet.

It's imperative that we provide needed opportunities for kids to develop the basics. When I speak on boys, I talk about how they should never spend more time in virtual reality than in real activity. Your son should never spend more time playing *Madden NFL 12* than actually throwing a football outside in the backyard. He should never spend more time texting than having actual conversations, developing the skills we just discussed earlier. He won't be very successful in business or marriage if he can't have *real* conversations and work through *real* conflict in *real* time.

In the next section, we'll discuss other needed ingredients for developing *real* connection. These ingredients are designed to spark creativity and intentionality, not shame and guilt. If you find yourself thinking, *I'm a lousy parent, and I haven't done enough in this area,* avoid getting roadblocked in shame; instead, use it as a gentle reminder of the opportunity to jumpstart your connections.

Relationship

I had lunch with a friend (a real friend, not a Facebook friend) this week; he is the father of two young boys. He shared a story

of being at a park with his sons recently and watching his son
Max climb on a metal railing. Max was climbing the railing,
twisting his body in and out like a human pretzel. My friend
watched in amazement as Max moved from being sideways to
upside down, vertical to horizontal, and front facing to backward. Each time their eyes met, Max encouraged his dad to "give
it a try."

My friend responded by saying, "Max, when I was your age,
I loved doing things like that."

Young Max paused and innocently looked at his father and
said, "It still might be fun."

Max's words are an invitation. An invitation to play. An invitation to relationship. An invitation into connection.

Sometimes our children invite us directly, sometimes not.
Sometimes we miss the invitation because we aren't paying
attention, are distracted by life or work, are consumed with
some project or agenda, or are trapped in our own emotions.

Being connected involves listening and looking for the invitation. As I write these words, I'm seated next to a set of parents
sitting across the table from their teenage son. His hair is messy
and disheveled. He's wearing an old T-shirt and jeans. His parents are in dress clothes. My suspicion is that they are headed
to church. It's Sunday morning and they are having breakfast
together at this really cool coffeehouse in Nashville. The food
here is a nice way to get a cranky teenage boy out of bed on
a Sunday morning, and to make the experience of church go
down a little easier. They have strategically trapped him into
conversation (and connection) with chocolate chip muffins and
mochas. When he gets up to go to the bathroom, I'm thinking
about high-fiving them.

They laugh together from time to time. They seem to go back and forth between topics, something surface to something more serious. OK, I confess that I did listen in on their conversation. I heard the dad say, "Let's talk about getting your license in a couple of months." The boy got this huge smile on his face and said, "Let's do." Conversations about *all* things happen better with chocolate as one of the ingredients, in my opinion. These are wise, creative parents, working hard to maintain connection during a particularly difficult season of development.

Do you see the ingredients involved in this time of connecting? Creativity (the time, the food, a cool coffeehouse), laughter (mixed with heavy topics), and enjoyment.

We forget the importance of mixing in these ingredients as we journey forward in parenting. We can get so set on instruction, teaching, correction, and discipline that we forget the importance of enjoyment, laughter, and creativity. They don't have to be mutually exclusive of one another.

When I was younger, I read a wonderful memoir by Homer Hickam Jr. called *Rocket Boys*. It's Homer's story of growing up in a mining town and being destined to work in the mines when he had a passion for space and a hobby of shooting off rockets.

Homer pursued this passion, despite a lack of understanding or support from most of the people around him. He had a small group of buddies who shared this passion, a teacher who loved and believed in him, and a desire to see it through. He would go on to work for NASA and change the course of space travel. His story was made into a movie called *October Sky*. I share a scene from the film when I speak to parents on enjoyment and connection. The scene opens around the kitchen table on Homer's birthday. He is opening gifts from his family, and his mother is working to create this time of celebration. The celebration breaks open when his dad gives in to emotion and begins lecturing him about taking an interest in his own town instead of wasting time on rockets and space. The conversation turns to yelling and ends with his dad taking a work call and Homer storming out of the house, slamming doors and escaping his home.

Two scenes later, Homer is found standing in front of his father's desk, asking if he'd reconsider coming to see him shoot off a rocket that afternoon. Members of the town are gathering to celebrate the launching, yet Homer longs for his dad to be present. He asks his dad why he never has work when Jim, his brother, is playing football. His dad appears trapped by the question and asks what time the launch takes place.

To watch this scene is to feel this young man's ache for connection and validation. He is desperate for his dad's approval and attention. You feel it in every word. It's the same invitation young Max gave his father: come be with me. Homer's father is trapped in his work, his agenda, his emotion, and his own ideas about who his son should be. These traps serve as obstacles to connection.

When I share this scene in classes, I often counter it with another scene. It's from a film based on a book called *Eat, Pray, Love* by Elizabeth Gilbert. In this scene, Liz and Felipe are hiking in the mountains with his nineteen-year-old son. Felipe is hiking ahead of them, taunting them with playful comments like, "You're moving like turtles. My grandmother hikes faster than the two of you, but she's already dead." They are laughing together, bantering back and forth.

The son tells Liz a story of being ten and his father dropping him off for school and kissing him good-bye. He speaks of how embarrassing it was in front of his friends. She asks the question, "Why didn't you ask him to stop?" He comments, "Well, I did, but then I realized how happy it made the old guy, and I just gave in." They talk together until they stop at a breathtaking lookout and take in the beauty of what is around them.

The next scene involves the son packing the car to head back to college following the visit. The dad says, "The time was too short." He hugs his son, hands him some music he compiled for the car ride, and then forces some money into his hand. While doing so, he is talking with his son about how dangerous girls can be and giving advice on dating. It's a beautiful mixture of instruction and relationship.

His eyes fill with tears. The boy hugs Liz and then turns to his dad to say, "Well, don't I get a kiss?"

He and his father laugh together; he kisses the young man and hugs him again. He walks to his car, and the father stands weeping, evidence of his great love for this boy.

He looks to Liz and says he knows it's foolish to weep this way as the boy is turning into a man, but he can't help himself. It's a beautiful picture of connection and relationship, a strong contrast to Homer and his father.

Two young men, hungry for validation and connection. One father who sees this and one who doesn't.

Our journey toward being a connected parent involves watching and listening for the invitation to play. The invitation to relationship. The invitation to connection.

"It still might be fun."

Interest

As we consider what can be learned from studying these fathers and sons, it's important to note how desperately Homer wanted his father to acknowledge and celebrate his passion. He challenged his father's "need to work" when he had so little difficulty engaging with his brother's passion for football.

We don't get to choose our children's passions any more than we get to choose their hair color, eye color, or temperament. The great work God started is one that He is faithfully completing as our kids grow and develop. Our job is to study their design, their development, their temperaments, and their passions, and to nurture them in the way *they* should go, as Proverbs 22:6 so wisely instructs.

Homer's dad was making desperate attempts to thwart his son's passion and to direct his path according to what *he* believed to be right for him. To know Homer's story and the great contributions he made to history is to celebrate that his father was unsuccessful in his attempts to reshape Homer's future.

What does your son love?

What are your daughter's passions?

When do your kids seem most alive?

My daughter, like many little girls, fell in love with baby dolls at an early age. Some of my first books were written with a publisher in Chicago, and I traveled there to meet with my editor and team multiple times a year. I took my daughter with me on several trips. We'd carve out an extra day to ride a carriage around the city, stop for sundaes at the Ghirardelli Soda Shop on the Magnificent Mile, and then hit the American Girl Place, which, for a little girl, is the equivalent of me going to the Apple Store—glory as far as the eye can see.

The American Girl store allows parents and girls to eat in the café together while your doll dines beside you in her own special high chair. You can have hair done in the salon, purchase a matching wardrobe (daughter and doll, not dad and daughter), and drop hundreds of dollars in a matter of minutes. Needless to say, I have strongly supported the folks at the American Girl Place over the years. I suspect I've nearly paid the mortgage for the Chicago store in a few months.

Every time our family has expanded to include a new member—Kit, Josefina, Molly, or whoever the girl of the year is—we have a celebration. I've participated in dozens of tea parties while dressed in my finest to welcome the newest member of the Thomas family. I learned early on that it was disappointing to my daughter when I addressed one of the members of the family by the wrong name. If I accidentally said, "Kit, would you pass me a cupcake?" when I was seated next to Jane, it was deeply troubling to my daughter. She would kindly but strongly correct me with, "Dad, she's not paying attention to you because her name is Jane. Kit has on the yellow dress with flowers." I would immediately ask Jane's forgiveness and make my request again.

This may sound silly to you, but at that moment in her development, these dolls were her little world and held importance to her. Because my daughter is so important to me, her world is important to me. Important enough to wear a navy blazer to a tea party with American Girl dolls. It's a way of saying that the things that matter to her matter to me.

What matters in the lives of your children right now?

How could you build a deeper connection by exploring that world with them?

Safety

My daughter has grown beyond her love of the American Girl dolls. She's a tween now, and her interests have moved into other areas. The dolls are still on a shelf in her room, but they don't have her attention the way the new iPad she got for her birthday does. She loves books, friends, movies, music, and all the things girls love when they are in the throes of adolescence.

Rather than tea parties, now we go to coffeehouses and read books together. We, like many millions of readers, read *The Hunger Games*. We had great conversations about the characters and themes within those stories. We talked about courage and sacrifice, oppression and privilege, family and community.

We have a rule in our house that you can never see a film based on a book unless you've first read the book. We read the first book aloud to one another and finished days before the movie released. My wife caught us staying up after bedtime on a school night, squeezing in one more chapter.

Opening weekend finally rolled around, and we battled the crowds to see the film at a Saturday matinee. We purchased our tickets and showed up to stand in line with the masses just to get a seat. As we were standing outside the theater, waiting behind the roped-off section for the attendants to open the doors, the line snaked around in front of us to accommodate the numbers. Directly in front of us stood an adolescent boy and his girlfriend. They looked to be about sixteen. We'd been standing for a while when the boy looked at his girlfriend and said, "Go get me an ICEE." She immediately snapped to attention as he handed her a ten-dollar bill instead of a five-dollar one.

Girl: "I don't need this much money."

Boy: "Yeah you do, I want a large."

Girl: "A large is so much money. Why don't you get a small or medium? It's a huge waste of money."

Boy: (Barking at her) "I said I want a large. Get me what I want!"

She appeared scared by his tone and turned to head to concessions. As she departed, he slid down the wall into a lying (not a sitting) position, frustrated and sulking that we weren't entering anytime soon. He was lounging across two-thirds of the hallway at this point. An attendant walked by and said, "Excuse me, sir, could you kindly move your legs? It will be difficult for those exiting the theater to get by, and it's actually a fire hazard to lie down in the hallway."

He looked disgruntled, rolled his eyes, and moved just his legs while moaning, "Whatever."

Let me pause here by commenting that I know this boy. I don't actually know *him*, but he is familiar to me. Sometimes this profiled young man shows up in my office—entitled, arrogant, full of bravado. This young man possibly has some disconnect with his parents and may be under-parented. He needs a bit more supervision, coaching, discipline, and an after-school or summer job that involves sweat, hard work, and a supervisor who will give him a swift kick in the rear.

Because I know this type of young man, the counselor in me wanted to give him some feedback right there in the hallway, but then I reminded myself that I am off the clock and on a date with my daughter. And there would be no quicker way to humiliate my preteen daughter than to start correcting a sixteen-year-old boy who is not my client.

Then I thought, *Well, I'm not on the clock, but I am a concerned parent, and as a father, I want to protect that young girl who is with him. I want to jerk him up off the floor and shove that ICEE down his Abercrombie T-shirt and sagging jeans.* I fantasized about lying and saying that I'm friends with her dad, that I just recorded their exchange on my iPhone, and that he is going to apologize to the girl while I record that for her father as well. Then I imagined dragging him by the collar of his shirt over to the attendant to apologize. Next, I would make him buy her any size ICEE she wants, right after he sweeps up the spilled popcorn, a way of repairing his relationship with the theater attendant.

I came to my senses again and decided I could use this as a teachable moment with my daughter. I turned toward her and whispered, "Did you notice anything about that boy and his girlfriend?"

She looked distraught and said, "He was so mean to her. He screamed at her in front of everyone." She paused, looked troubled, and then added, "And then he was mean to the guy working here, who was just doing his job."

She had been absorbing every bit of the scene.

I said, "You're right, sweetheart. You are so observant. What do you think that girl is feeling right now?"

We talked back and forth and had this rich conversation about relationships, about what might be going on with the girl, and what was going on with Mr. Abercrombie. I asked a lot of questions and tried to let her connect the dots. Some days I do this better than others, but I always believe that's where the real learning takes place. I don't want to fill in all the blanks for my kids.

I ended the conversation by saying to my daughter, "If you're ever on a date and the boy speaks to you that way, I want you to know that you can go to the bathroom with your purse and call me. I will come get you *any* day, *any*where. I won't ask questions. I just want you to know you have an out anytime you need it." I went on to say, "I will never be OK with any boy talking to you like that. You are way too valuable, and no guy is worth that."

I stopped talking and we stood there for a minute, watching his frightened girlfriend return with the large ICEE. He never thanked her for it; he never apologized for yelling. She just stood there in silence, looking at the floor.

My daughter then looked at me and whispered, "What would you do if you came to get me?" I was so struck by her question that it took me a minute. I looked at her lovely face and said, "I want you to feel protected more than anything." She smiled and looked away. I glanced over at Saggy Britches, and then I looked back at her. "I would find your boyfriend and introduce him to another side of me."

Part of the connection I hope to experience with my daughter is where we started with the tea parties and continued with the books and beverages—that she is a priority for me and always will be. I want her to know that she is safe in my presence, and that I am committed to protecting her. I hope to build connection with her that might somehow allow her to call me from the bathroom of a movie theater to come and get her if she ever feels unsafe in some circumstance.

I believe a part of that connection involves me promising I won't ask questions right then. If (or when) my daughter someday makes a decision she regrets and ends up at a party in the middle of a moment of failure, I want her to know it's safe to cry for help and she'd be met without judgment, without a lecture, and without shame.

I hope I have some sense of myself in that moment not to humiliate her, like I almost did at the theater. I hope I'm parenting out of love, not fear. I hope I'm parenting with emotion but not *out of* emotion. I hope I have the presence of mind to remember that the real connecting of the dots happens when she figures it out on her own, not when I fill in the blanks.

Ask your kids to tell you something they wish you did more
or less of as a parent. Think about turning their response into
valuable information that allows you to create more safety in
their experience of you as a parent.

Contentment

All of those things involve awareness. This book is full of reminders of the importance of being aware. We have so much more to offer our kids when we operate from a place of awareness—of our shortcomings and areas of deficit, of our triggers, of when we get needy and depleted, of when we need a break, of when our expectations are unrealistic, of when we are living vicariously through our children, and of when we need to ask for forgiveness.

I talked earlier about the importance of being interested in our kids, pursuing the things they love, and engaging their world. While this is vital to connection, we can actually go overboard in this pursuit. Sissy tells the story of running into an adolescent girl and her mom in Starbucks and the mom (in tears) reporting, "*We* just broke up with *her* boyfriend."

I know dads who chart their sons' batting averages and study footage of their games like recruiters. In their off time, they make protein smoothies, talk strategy, and require hours of practice at home outside of the required practice on the field. We can take our interest and involvement *too* far.

Similarly, we've known single parents who have unintentionally used their children as emotional spouses. They brought them into conversations about finances or frustrations with their ex-spouses.

Melissa speaks often about what happens when we get stuck in our own development and need our kids to like us or approve of us. These different traps all represent a lack of contentment in some area.

Contentment is an important ingredient in being a connected parent. It frees our kids up to be kids because they know we are being the grown-ups. Let me give you an example of this kind of contentment. Remember the mom who yelled, "Don't drink," in the dorm parking lot at drop-off her son's freshman year? Let me introduce you to a second mom in that same season of life.

This mom, in preparing to send her son off to college, shared this story with me. It was a couple of months before her son was due to head to college, and they'd been talking about this important transition for quite some time. One day her son walked through the kitchen while she was making dinner and glanced at a list of names taped to the fridge door. The list included MacK & Kate, Margot, Kay Bob, and Monell's. The young man paused and asked, "Who are all these people?"

She commented, "Actually, those are the names of restaurants across the city that your dad and I plan on visiting once you're away at school." The boy paused, not quite knowing how to respond to his parents' plan. The mom just smiled.

This mom will likely experience some of the same emotions the other mom experienced at drop-off. She is choosing not to let those emotions define how she cares for her son in his final months before heading off to school. I would say this wise mom is freeing him up from the responsibility of believing his presence determines her happiness. Put simply, she is having a life outside of him. Doing so is one of the healthiest gifts we can offer our kids.

We live in a very child-centered moment in history. We tend to elevate parents who are highly involved in their children's lives, activities, academics, and emotions. In a world of travel sports, private trainers, and tutors, parents are almost encouraged to orbit their children. We lose sight of the importance of being *people* who are also parents. We forget to spend time with our spouses and friends, and we drop hobbies and interests as if we're being selfish to maintain them.

This wise mom knew that posting the list of restaurants would allow her to think beyond her son leaving home. It ended up serving as a reminder to him that his parents will miss him when he leaves, but they will be OK. Actually *better* than OK, his mom won't cook as often and will enjoy trying new foods at gourmet restaurants.

On a practical level, it's important to infuse this priority into our parenting from early on. It could begin with having kids wait when you are taking a phone call, not giving them permission to interrupt you or demand your attention. It could advance from there to dinners with friends. Your children see you modeling the importance of having healthy friendships that nourish you. Kids within married homes need to see their parents go on dates and prioritize their marriage. Single parents need to model how important it is to refuel through whatever activities and relationships allow you to do so.

We'd even go as far as to encourage you to purposely miss some of your kids' games or activities when opportunities arise. They need to see you devote yourself to service, relationship, and opportunities that are important to your life emotionally, relationally, and spiritually.

Equally so, they need to see you connected to God and resting in the contentment we experience in that relationship—that we are known, loved, and protected.

Where can you prioritize and experience more life outside your children, as a means of creating more balance and communicating greater contentment as a person?

8.

Being an Encouraging Parent

—with Sissy

"CORRECTION DOES MUCH BUT ENCOURAGEMENT does more,"[1] said Goethe. We've talked a lot about the value of consistency. Consistency is important, but it is not enough. All of the consistency in the world, without encouragement, would create a compliant, lonely, lost child. Consistency teaches children how to act, but encouragement teaches them who they are.

We asked several kids, grades two through twelve, how they felt encouraged by their parents. These are their answers (in their words):

Second through fourth graders:

- When my mom says, "How was your day?"
- When my parents say, "You're so loving."

- When my parents tell me, "It's okay. You'll feel better."
- When my parents say, "Keep trying . . . You can do it!"
- When my parents say, "You are so smart."
- When my dad says, "You're my Irish genius girl!"
- When my parents stood up for me when I got blamed for something I didn't do.
- When my parents helped me calm down when I was mad!
- When my parents take me out for ice cream.
- When my parents tell me, "Good job."
- When my parents cheer me on and encourage me in swim team. That makes me feel special.
- When my dad helps me practice piano he can say really nice things.
- When I come home from school, my mom always encourages me. When I wake up, my mom encourages me just by being nice.

Fifth through sixth graders:

- When me and my mom do fun activities together.
- When my mom makes my favorite food.
- When my dad compliments my work.
- When my mom shows off my good grades.
- Being proud of me when I did the rope jump even though I was scared to do it.
- When I was sad, my mom made me very happy.
- When my dad says I'm a good artist.
- When my mom pays attention to me.
- When I was going to try out for cheerleading, my parents

said they thought I would do great and just do my best
and have fun!

- They help me out by comforting me.
- When they give me hugs!
- Taking me on one-on-one dates.
- Telling me, "You are beautiful, and there is nobody else
  that is like you."
- When they agree with me.
- At the marathon once, they cheered me on the whole
  time.
- When they hug and pray with me every night and
  whenever possible.
- When they let me cry on them when I'm upset.
- When they remind me of what I can do and why I'm
  special.
- When my dad yells at me for no reason, I talk to my
  mom about it and she tells me how to get over it.
- If I am having a fight with them and the fight is over,
  they tell me they love me no matter what.

Seventh through eighth graders:

- When my mom brought me my favorite drink after I
  visited a new school.
- When they take me to counseling.
- When they listen and are always there for me, even when
  I'm not talking about anything important.
- When they say they know I've tried my best.
- When my dad says, "I believe in you."
- When they send me encouraging texts.

- When they let me invite my friends over.
- When my dad helps me with basketball.
- When my mom takes me places like a concert or shopping.
- When they laugh with me about something funny.

High schoolers

- When they don't let me say I'm stupid.
- When my dad takes the day off just so we can have a "daddy/daughter day."
- When they give me freedom and don't treat me like a child.
- When they take the time to talk to me like an adult.
- Being there for me.
- Understanding.
- When my mom said that any college that doesn't accept me is stupid.
- When I didn't get something I wanted, my mom told me she was so proud of me anyway.
- When my dad tells me he's proud of me when I try something new.
- Even when they're telling me something I need to work on, they still say something positive.
- When I mess up, my dad tells me he still loves me, which always makes me feel so much better about my mistakes.

If your son or daughter made a list of the ways you encourage him or her, what would be on it?

What would he say happens when he messes up?

What would she remember that you've told her about who she is?

I was recently speaking at a conference for children's ministers when a young woman came up to me obviously burdened. "Can I talk to you?" she said with tears in her eyes, and beckoned me to a corner. She had a raw, artsy, slightly unkempt look about her, making her seem more like she was a high school student pushing her parents' boundaries, than a young woman living out the story she told. "I was just standing at your book table, flipping through *Raising Girls*, when I came to the end where it talks about naming. My mind immediately switched from the lives of the kids I work with to my own. It made me think about my dad. When I was growing up, he named me a slut. Not just once, but a lot. Since then, I've had sex with nine different guys. Now, I'm a single mom. I still hear his words in my head constantly. I feel like he was right. I am a slut. I keep trying to be different, but I don't know how."

Your words, as a parent, have more power in the life of your child than anyone else's most likely ever will. They set the course for how your child will see him- or herself for years. In offices throughout the world, counselors and therapists talk about the "tapes" we hear in our heads, filling us with self-doubt. It is often the voices of our parents that make up those tapes.

I know a mom of two teenagers who is one of the most encouraging individuals I've ever known. I recently said this to her, in front of her children. Her immediate reply was, "Not really . . . ask them. I might be good at encouraging other people, but I'm afraid I'm not so good with my own kids." She turned to them and said, "Would you all agree?" Her daughter quietly said, "Well, you spend a lot of time telling us what we need to work on." The mom turned back to me, with regret in her eyes, and said, "See?"

Encouragement is many things, which we'll talk about throughout this chapter. But your children will potentially be the hardest people in your life to encourage. You will, naturally, at times. But at other times, it will feel next to impossible. The true nature of encouragement gets cloudy when you're a parent. It gets mixed up with other thoughts and feelings. You're with them constantly. They know how to push your buttons. You see the areas in which they need to grow and feel it's your duty to push them. They also feel like an extension of who you are in a way that can sometimes make you critical. The father in the earlier story could have been misguidedly trying to encourage his daughter to make better choices. This mom really wanted to encourage her kids, but often saw their weaknesses more than their strengths. Encouragement is not criticism. It's not pruning your child as you would a bush with scraggly branches. As a matter of fact, let's start with what encouragement isn't, before we move on to the promising truth of what encouragement is.

Encouragement Is Not . . .

CRITICISM. Criticism can take many forms. It can be outright, like calling your children names. It can also take the form of a backhanded compliment. "It's nice to see you finally cleaning your room. I knew you had it in you." To a child, criticism can also feel like a parent who is relentlessly pushing her to do better. Ephesians 4:29 says, "Do not let any unwholesome talk come out of your mouths, but only what is helpful for building others up according to their needs, that it may benefit those who listen" (NIV). *The Message* translation of the same verse ends with, "Say only what helps, each word a gift." Criticism is never a gift. Backhanded compliments don't benefit those who listen. Neither does pushing them relentlessly to do better. These tactics just make your child feel worse. Think about offering your words as a gift to your kids, a gift that builds them up. Your son and your daughter need you to reflect the good you see in them, by your words and your actions, without any negative subtext.

MINIMIZING. Minimizing sounds like a strong word. You may read it and think, *I wouldn't do that to my child.* But minimizing statements are sentences we often say with the best of intentions. We use them to soften the blow, such as, "It's really not all that bad," or "You're making a much bigger deal of this than it is." We say them when our kids are reenacting the proverbial "making mountains out of molehills." Kids do make mountains out of molehills. Or, at least their mountains look like molehills to us. But they are *their* mountains. They need us to honor them as such. They need us to listen and hear them in a way in which they feel understood. Our attempts to make them feel better by minimizing the situation just serve to stop them from sharing their feelings with us.

SARCASM. Girls want to connect with their dads. Dads want to connect with their daughters. It's the same way with sons. Sometimes, joking around seems like the easiest entry point for connection. But sarcasm is just that . . . easy. It's cheap and easy in a way that leaves both parties feeling empty and even sometimes hurt. We all believe that laughter is a necessity to the life of your family, but never at the expense of a family member. Sarcasm often reduces itself to that. Dads, you are, at times, in your lighthearted way, the one most susceptible to falling into the sarcastic trap. Don't be fooled by your son's or daughter's willingness to joke back. Sarcasm hurts. Your kids may not tell you, but they tell us behind the closed doors of our offices.

COMPARING. Bill Cosby's routine about walking to school both ways uphill in the snow is funny to us, but it wouldn't be to your son or daughter. One teenage girl I meet with tells me how often her mom compares her childhood to her daughter's. "I would never have _____ when I was a kid," she says. It can be about disrespect, entitlement, or any other issue kids deal with differently today than in the way-back-whens. For this girl, her mom's comments make her feel as if her mom is saying, "When I was a teenager, I was perfect. I was better . . . or kinder . . . or more responsible than you." It makes her feel that her mom sees her as "less than". And once again, the communication breaks down. You may think, *I'd never say anything like that to my child.* But you might to a friend. Beware that children hear and pick up on far more than we realize, especially when it pertains to them.

QUICK ADVICE. "If you would just talk to your teacher, the whole problem would be solved." When your child presents you with a problem he's experiencing, you'll often know just what he should do. And you'll frequently come up with the solution three sentences into his explanation of the problem. But he needs you to wait. He wants you to listen. He needs you to help him come up with the solution, not just fix the problem for him.

COMPENSATING. It takes five positive comments to make up for one negative. Or ten positive comments, or even twenty, depending on the source. Encouragement is not a means to compensate for a critical remark that slipped out when your child made a mistake. Don't try to cover your wrong by saying something kind about her. Instead, respect her enough to apologize. When you apologize, your child learns how to forgive and accept herself when she fails. Then, encourage her out of a genuine place of love, rather than guilt.

MANIPULATION. "I know you can lose the weight you want."

"Mom, I'm not even worried about losing weight. You're the one who wants me to lose weight. Not me!"

I have had some version of this conversation many times with girls and moms over the years. Sometimes it's said out loud, and sometimes it's just hinted at through side comments and "encouragement." We can all fall into this category. We want to see the people we love succeed. We want to see them grow in areas in which we believe they struggle. And so we subtly push. Pushing can be a great thing when we know we're pushing them toward something *they* want but may be afraid to pursue. But when that something is what *we* want more than they do, it becomes manipulation.

Which of these obstacles to encouragement do you most often fall into?

How do you believe it affects your child?

At times, our attempts to encourage will look more like what encouragement isn't than what it truly is. When that happens, not *if*, it will affect our communication with our kids, as well as their confidence in themselves and in us. It is in those moments that we cling to what encouragement is. And true encouragement has much more to do with the posture of our hearts than the slip-ups we make as sinful, but well-meaning, parents.

Encouragement Is . . .

In their book *Encouragement*, Larry Crabb and Dan Allender define *encouragement* as "not a technique to be mastered; it is a sensitivity to people and a confidence in God that must be nourished and demonstrated."[2]

If we were to restate their terms specific to parenting, it would be something like this: "Encouragement is not a technique to be mastered; it is a sensitivity to your child's heart and a confidence in God as protector, provider, and redeemer that must be leaned into and reflected to your child."

So, what does this mean? We normally think of encouragement as a kind word spoken when someone is in need. As parents, encouragement runs much deeper. It requires more of who you are and offers more of who they can be.

Encouragement Requires . . .

OBJECTIVITY. "I need two things from you today. First, I need you to help me decide if my daughter should change schools. Second, I need you to help me get off the roller coaster." This insightful mom knew that she was struggling with one of the principles necessary to encouragement. "It's like she's on this perpetual roller coaster," she said. "Up and down, up and down, almost on a daily basis. I want so much to help, but I jump on that thing right beside her, and then I'm just as emotional as she is." Encouragement requires objectivity. Girls tell me, at times, that their parents seem more hurt or angry over a situation in their lives than they do. Maybe they've been hurt by a friend or not made it onto a certain team. In those situations, they end up feeling like they can't talk to their parents. Boys feel much the same. When they sense us rising up emotionally, they shrink back. And as we rise up and feel hurt or angry or slighted on their behalf, our feelings cloud our judgment. Objectivity allows us to hear *their* feelings and remain clear-minded as we help them work through *their* issues.

DISCERNMENT. In Crabb and Allender's book, they have another thought that feels particularly applicable in being an encouraging parent: encouragement is "1) inspired by love, and 2) directed toward fear."[3] When we're talking about your child, you've got the love part down. It comes with the territory of parenting. And even on days when your child irritates you, there is still a foundational love that God instills in the heart of every parent. If it weren't there, you wouldn't have picked up this book. It's the fear we want to speak to more directly. At any given moment, your child is experiencing some type of fear. There are fears kids say out loud, such as, "I don't want you to fall asleep before I do," or "I don't know how to drive a car." There are also unspoken fears, like going to camp without any friends, or that you, their parents, might get divorced. And then there are fears that lurk so deep that they're unknown even to your children. These fears can affect their actions and their views on life and God. Your kids need you to listen with discernment. They need you to hear what they're sometimes not even saying and speak to those fears.

PERSISTENCE. To listen in the way we're describing requires persistence. It means that you take the time and energy to stop and hear what your child's truly saying to you. It means that you watch his behaviors, that you notice when she becomes shy or unsure of herself. It means that you reflect on what it would feel like to be him . . . at school, at church, even at home. He needs you to ask the deeper questions. And then, if he doesn't answer, ask again at another time. He may not answer, but he knows that you care enough about him that you want to hear.

OPTIMISM. Encouragement exists only within the realm of positivity. When I am critical or negative or have a pessimistic view on life, which I do way too often, it is impossible for me to be encouraging. Everything starts to look bleak. And my bleakness seeps over into the lives of those I love. To offer true encouragement to your son, he needs you to believe the best about him, about life, and about God. He needs you to believe he is capable and to reflect that belief to him. He needs to know you truly believe things will get better. And that is never more difficult to believe than when your child is hurting. In those times, the only hope we can have or offer comes through faith.

FAITH. The most important requirement of encouragement is undoubtedly faith. Without faith—in who your child is, in who you are as a parent, and ultimately in a God who loves each of you more than you could imagine—encouragement falls short. Faith brings objectivity, discernment, persistence, and optimism together in a way that enables you to speak truth into the darkness for and with your child.

I think of faith as a kind of whistling in the dark because, in much the same way, it helps to give us courage and to hold the shadows at bay. To whistle in the dark isn't to pretend that the dark doesn't sometimes scare the living daylights out of us. Instead, I think, it's to demonstrate, if only to ourselves, that not even the dark can quite overcome our trust in the ultimate triumph of the Living Light.[4]

The Living Light will triumph when your son has been bullied. He will triumph when your daughter is depressed. You can trust in a God who is good and who redeems every struggle your family will go through. Your daughter needs you to believe that for her . . . and for you. And then, she needs you to grab her hand and teach her what it means to whistle. That is what true encouragement looks like.

Encouragement Offers . . .

She sat on my couch for the sixth time in the past two months. Her mom was waiting downstairs to come up and have yet another mother/daughter session. They weren't going well. Each week, we basically had the same conversation with the same conclusion. This mom and her teenage daughter needed to learn to enjoy each other. Instead, the daughter looked sad and resigned. I tried to be positive.

"Have you all spent any time together in the last week?" I asked cheerily.

"Yeah," she said, not so cheerily. "We went to dinner together before this. We didn't talk the whole time. There's no point."

Trying to offer a little levity and hope, I said, "There's always a point."

"Not with her," she immediately responded. "She just doesn't like me."

As a counselor with nineteen years of experience working with kids, I believe what this daughter needs desperately is encouragement from her mom. She needs to know that her mom believes in her, at a time when she doesn't believe much in herself. She needs to hear positive things spoken about her to her by one of the most influential people in her life. She longs to be enjoyed by her mom. And because her mom is more aware of and speaks to what her daughter is doing wrong rather than right, her daughter has given up.

Encouragement offers hope. It offers life and healing. And it offers a relationship that keeps you connected to your children in a way that helps them believe the truth of Philippians 1:6: "Being confident of this, that he who began a good work in you will carry it on to completion until the day of Christ Jesus" (NIV).

When your son is bullied on the playground, he may not believe that a good work is being done in him. When your daughter fails a science test . . . when your nine-year-old is too anxious to stay at school . . . when your teenager struggles with self-doubt, they need you to be their reminder that God has begun a good work. They need your words spoken to the good you see and your actions that back up your words. They desperately need your encouragement.

RELATIONSHIP. Adolescence is a time when your relationship with your child will be particularly strained. Son or daughter—it doesn't matter. In teens' journey to become independent, they will often push against you the hardest. It's natural, but it's not enjoyable, for either of you. Encouragement, in those times, will help you maintain relationship. Take every opportunity you can to stop teaching or correcting and simply encourage. In his book *Blue Like Jazz*, Donald Miller said, "No one will listen to you unless they sense that you like them."[5] This is particularly true for teens of their parents. Encouragement communicates your enjoyment of and belief in them. It also strengthens the bond you once shared and will share again when the strains of this season end.

LIFE. "The tongue has the power of life and death, and those who love it will eat its fruit" (Prov. 18:21 NIV). Have you ever seen your child lose his or her sense of life? He pours all of his time, energy, and creativity into a painting, only to have someone make a negative comment about it. It's as if you can see the light go out of his eyes. Your daughter doesn't get asked to prom, and she mopes around the house for days, looking lost and dejected. They lose their life, and they lose it so easily. Your children will encounter words of death in countless venues—on the playground, on the soccer field, at sleepovers, and on dates. They will hear plenty of words that hurt and drain the life and confidence from them. They need something different from you. In these times, and in ordinary times, they need you to use words that are motivated by love and directed toward their fears. They need the person who knows them best to offer words that bring the life and power of which these verses in Proverbs speak.

HEALING. "Kind words heal and help; cutting words wound and maim" (Prov. 15:4 MSG). "Pleasant words are a honeycomb, sweet to the soul and healing to the bones" (Prov. 16:24 NIV). Today's kids are hurting. According to kidshealth.org, 1 in every 33 children may struggle with depression. For teenagers, as many as 1 in 8.[6] Anxiety disorders plague more than

13 percent of today's children.[7] Sixty percent of middle schoolers report being bullied.[8] And those statistics just include the
kids who are talking about it. Melissa and I recently spoke at
a mother/daughter retreat at one of the top girls' camps in the
country. After a session with the girls, the director turned to us
and said, "The problems kids are facing today are more complex
than ever before." This is spoken by someone who has worked
with girls for more than twenty years. We would agree completely. We see the complexity of those problems day in and day
out at Daystar. Your words can help aid the healing and preven-
tion of those issues and more in your children. Words, however,
are not a fix-all. At times, encouragement is not enough. But
your words will help your depressed son see that he is more
than just his sadness. Your words to your hurting daughter can
help her know that this, too, shall pass. Whether the situation is
big or small, your words have the power to bring healing. And
when the words don't feel like enough, they can point your child
to the Healer, who is redeeming all things for His glory.

TRUTH. Think back on your growing-up years. What did
you believe was true about you? How much was because someone else spoke it into being in your mind? In Genesis, God used
words to create. "Let there be light." And there was. "Let there
be land and waters and vegetation and man." And there was.
Words have the power to create, even in your child's self-image.
In Kelly Corrigan's book *The Middle Place*, she speaks about the
encouragement her dad offered her as a child:

> He told me once that I was a great talker. And so I was. I was
> a conversationalist, along with creative, a notion he put in
> my head when I was in grade school and used to make huge,

intricate collages from his old magazines. He defined me first, as parents do. Those early characterizations can become the shimmering self-image we embrace or the limited, stifling perception we rail against for a lifetime. In my case, he sees me as I would like to be seen. In fact, I'm not even sure what's true about me, since I have always chosen to believe his version.[9]

Your voice is different from anyone else's in your child's life. You have the power—or, even better, the honor—to speak truth to your children about who they are in a way that defines them. What version are you communicating? How do you want them to see themselves, and how can you communicate those truths in a way that makes them feel encouraged?

HOPE. "For in this hope we were saved. But hope that is seen is no hope at all. Who hopes for what he already has? But if we hope for what we do not yet have, we wait for it patiently" (Rom. 8:24–25 NIV).

Of all the things encouragement offers your child, hope is perhaps the most important. The tagline for our book *Mirrors and Maps* is "grace for who you are and hope for who you're becoming." As you encourage your children, you give them this kind of grace and hope. But you also point them to a hope that runs much deeper. Each child will place his or her hope in a lot of things over the years—new friends, parts in plays, winning football teams, homecoming dates, SAT scores. And when those things fall through, discouragement will follow. Your encouragement, in those times, is invaluable. A middle school girl I meet with said that her mom puts a new scripture on her mirror every day . . . just to encourage her. A high school girl told me how much it means when she knows her mom is praying specifically for her and for what she's facing that day. The encouragement of these moms is a genuine expression of their hope. When your encouragement rises out of that place, it has more impact than you can imagine.

In all of the complexities of growing up today, children and teens need hope. They need life and healing and relationship with you, as their parent. And they need you to offer these things out of the overflow of your heart. Encouragement is not just the words you say. It's not just the truth and hope that you offer. It's the way you live God's truth and God's hope out. Sensitivity to your child's heart and confidence in God as your protector, provider, and redeemer is what truly encourages. You offer hope as you point your children toward Christ.

Several years ago, I was riding my bike in our annual Bike Thing, a fund-raising event for the families at Daystar who can't afford the full cost of counseling. We had ridden twenty miles and were on the last stretch. I was exhausted. We had just finished a long, glorious downhill and reached the foot of a climb that looked as if it stretched for miles. As I started up, I noticed a father and daughter in front of me. She was probably twelve years old and riding in that awkward, twisting-your-handlebars way that you ride when you just can't pedal up another hill. Her dad, who was behind her, quickly came alongside. He placed his left hand on her back, with his right hand on his own handlebars. And for the remainder of that hill, he pushed. He rode beside her and kept his hand on her back with just enough pressure to keep her going. And more than enough to remind her that he was there.

How could you intentionally encourage your child more?

Encouragement awakens the heart of your children and enlivens their faith, both in themselves and in God's good work that He's completing in them. Don't give up. If nothing else, you have all that you need to place your hand on your child's back, because your Father has placed His hand on yours.

So let's do it—full of belief, confident that we're presentable inside and out. Let's keep a firm grip on the promises that keep us going. He always keeps his word. Let's see how inventive we can be in encouraging love and helping out, not avoiding worshiping together as some do but spurring each other on, especially as we see the big Day approaching. (Heb. 10:22–25 MSG)

Putting It into Practice . . .

- Focus on his strengths.
- Notice her effort, regardless of the outcome.
- Give her a chance to contribute.
- Help him take small, achievable steps toward his goals, and celebrate his accomplishments.
- Laugh with her.
- Listen.
- Speak to the fear that may be underneath his words.
- Play together, no matter what her age.
- Say thank you.
- Apologize.
- Do something special for your daughter as a surprise.
- Tell him you love him. Often.

9.

Being a Spiritual Parent

—with Melissa

I am reminded that I cannot be Jesus; I can only need Jesus. In the times when I feel as though I fail most—when I dissolve before my children into anger or helplessness—He comes and forgives my exhaustion, sin, and limitations. He teaches me that His own work in my children's lives is not dependent upon me, that even in my weakness I'm living out before my children the most essential truth of our lives: all of us are in severe need of this glorious and merciful Savior.[1]

I am pretty simple. I like to keep things simple and describe things simply. You would know that if you were around Daystar in the early days. We had a bike fund-raiser. I called it the Bike Thing. We had events on Monday nights. I called them the

Monday Night Things. Our Christmas fund-raiser was almost called the Christmas Thing, but instead ended up being An Evening in December. I guess I just kind of call things as they are.

So, to me, this chapter is simple as well. Not that we're going to call it the Spiritual Thing. But I believe we complicate what being spiritual looks like. We often make it a to-do list of what we think is required to be a godly parent. I believe being a spiritual parent has more to do with who you are than what you do—and who you are is a person (and parent) who severely needs Jesus.

Dependent Parenting

At a parenting seminar several years ago, Sissy brought a group of teenage girls for the question-and-answer segment at the end of the class. One mom in the audience asked the girls, "What is something your mom has done for you as you've grown up that's kept you connected to her?" One senior in high school responded immediately. "Every morning, when I come downstairs, I see my mom reading her Bible and writing in her prayer journal. We never talked about it, but it's had a major effect on our relationship; it's helped me feel safe and like I could trust her."

I spoke with this mom a few days later and told her what her daughter said. Her response was honest and unassuming. "I do that because I have to. It's not that I choose to have a quiet time every morning because I'm trying to be a godly example for my daughter, although I do want to be that. I read my Bible and spend time praying because I'm compelled to. I don't have a choice. Raising a child is too hard. I just can't do it alone."

Eugene Peterson said, "The parent's main task is to be

vulnerable in a living demonstration that adulthood is full, alive, and Christian."[2] Being vulnerable is difficult when you're a parent, especially a spiritual parent. You are "supposed to be" strong, together, in control. But the reality, to put it simply, is that you're not.

At a mother/daughter conference, Sissy and I were on a panel in front of more than one thousand women. I was asked the question, "Can you tell me the secret to making sure my child grows up to be Christ-centered and well-rounded?" I turned to the audience, smiled, and said with all of the wisdom and warmth I could muster, "No."

I can't. But the question has intrigued me ever since. What do you hear underneath it? Do you hear the fear (*"the secret"—no one has told me it so far, and I need you to*)? Do you hear the need for control ("... making sure my child grows up to be ...")? Do you hear the lack of trust? (Why does "well-rounded" follow "Christ-centered"? Shouldn't being Christ-centered be enough?) I hear those things because I've seen them in myself . . . all too often.

Our fears, the need for control, for guarantees, even for things to be like we think they should, all stifle our vulnerability. Vulnerability involves a letting go of control. It means there are no guarantees, that we're giving up control over what we think should happen.

It is only as a Christian that I believe we can. We can let go because it is God who takes up. We can give up what we think should happen because what will happen is in His control rather than ours anyway. And we know that in all things God works for the good of those who love Him—parents and children alike—who have been called according to His purpose. (His purpose, not ours; it's in Romans 8:28.)

So, let's go ahead and get it out in the open. You are vulnerable. Even if you're one of the parents others see as strong, godly, and together. You and I know the truth. You're vulnerable. You're dependent. You need God severely. And that's exactly what your children need from you.

What do you feel when you read the words "dependent parenting"?

How would your children describe your relationship with God?

Growing Up in Christ

Parenting is a great paradox. You spend more than eighteen years raising your children to leave. You invest energy and time and hope and patience and love, so much love, helping them discover who they are, to find their own voice in this world. All of the time you, in essence, are growing right alongside your children. And the paradox is that while they are growing up into a state of independence, you are growing more dependent on God.

Paul, in Ephesians 4, wrote about maturing in Christ:

Then we will no longer be infants, tossed back and forth by the waves, and blown here and there by every wind of teaching and by the cunning and craftiness of people in their deceitful scheming. Instead, speaking the truth in love, we will grow to become in every respect the mature body of him who is the head, that is, Christ. From him the whole body, joined and

held together by every supporting ligament, grows and builds
itself up in love, as each part does its work. (vv. 14–16 NIV)

This picture of being tossed back and forth, blown here and
there by cunning and craftiness, can be very descriptive of parenting. I would imagine your children have been cunning and
crafty from time to time—and you, as a parent, have felt blown
here and there. The mom in the earlier story did. That is why her
daughter saw her reading her Bible every day. It was because she
needed it, rather than because it was something she was supposed to do. It was a response to her need and her relationship
with God. Growing up in Christ is marked, primarily, by our
dependence on Him.

To put it simply, once again, spiritual parents need Jesus.
Their faith is rooted in God, rather than their godly parenting. Their actions—your actions—are based on the overflow
of God's goodness to you, rather than your good behavior. You
have a quiet time because you trust Christ and crave His near-
ness. You have a sense of gratitude, not just so you can model it
for your children, but because He has met you, time and time
again, in your need. You pray, not because it's the right thing to
do, but because you are seeking God's voice to guide you. What
you do is a response to who you are, as a spiritual parent. And
spiritual parents are many things, in response to all they have
received.

Spiritual Parents Respond by Being . . .

IN GOD'S WORD. Yes, it is good for your children to see
you reading your Bible. It models for them the importance of
being in the Word. But much more important for you is the

strength that God gives you through His Word. He speaks to you, offering wisdom and hope in times when parenting can feel hopeless and your own wisdom seems to run dry. His Word does not return void (paraphrase, Isaiah 55:11).

IN COMMUNITY. Parenting, at times, is a lonely, isolating task. When we become lonely, we often believe those myths like, "All the other parents have it together," or "None of the other parents feel this frustrated and disconnected from their children." Community can be a shared vulnerability that frees you to parent out of truths, rather than myths. Find a small group of believers with whom you can share your parenting struggles and failures. It needs to be a group where you're not afraid of gossip and judgment. If there isn't a small group at your church, start one and be the first to be vulnerable. It will create an atmosphere of openness that will free others to do the same. And you will be reminded that you're not alone as a parent, but in community with other broken, sinful, failing parents who are all desperately in need of God (Matthew 18:20).

IN PRAYER. Parenting in today's world can keep you moving at a frenetic pace. When you are in prayer regularly, God slows you down. You have time to listen and reflect. Be still. Silent. Say out loud to Him the worries that bounce around endlessly inside of you. As you do, His Spirit has an opportunity to refresh you in the deeper places of your spirit. He comes in and whispers words of love, joy, and hope to the parts of you that are worried, hurt, and afraid (1 Kings 19:11–12). Prayer is, in equal parts, us expressing our hearts to God and then Him moving in and through our hearts to refill us in ways only He can. Madeline L'Engle put it this way:

Prayer will take my words and then reveal their emptiness. The stilled voice learns to hold its peace, to listen with the heart to silence that is joy, is adoration. The self is shattered, all words torn apart in this strange patterned time of contemplation that, in time, breaks time, breaks words, breaks me, and then, in silence, leaves me healed and mended.[3]

GRATEFUL. Spiritual parents are grateful. They have a gratitude that emanates from the joy of knowing they are loved. That they're not alone. That they're wrapped in and covered by God's mercy on a daily basis. Rather than just teaching their children lessons on gratitude, their gratitude spills over into the lives of their family. It's infectious in a way that God describes in Jeremiah:

Thanksgivings will pour out of the windows; laughter will spill through the doors. Things will get better and better. Depression days are over. They'll thrive, they'll flourish. The days of contempt will be over. They'll look forward to having children again, to being a community in which I take pride. (Jeremiah 30:19–20 MSG)

Gratitude is infectious, and it naturally invites others to join in. Something as simple as saying, "Isn't this a beautiful day?" invites others to a place of gratitude. Try it. Be intentionally grateful with your children.

DISCERNING. "And it is my prayer that your love may abound more and more, with knowledge and all discernment." (Phil. 1:9 ESV). Spiritual parents understand that there is a time for all things. There is a time to speak and a time to be silent. There is a time to teach and a time to allow your children to discover truth for themselves. Spiritual parents are able to parent from a place of understanding—understanding both who your children are and what they need from you, at different ages and different times.

TRUSTING. Every parent who comes to Daystar is afraid. They are afraid of what will happen to their child if _____. It could be "if their father leaves," "if her sister dies," "if she changes to a new school and still isn't accepted," "if he can't pull his grades up in time." When you have the love that you do for these little people, accompanied by your deep desire to protect them, your life can be full of *ifs*. Most parents have a parade of *ifs* that march through their minds as they lie in bed at night. But what sets spiritual parents apart is their sense of trust. Jesus said:

> "What I'm trying to do here is get you to relax, not be so preoccupied with getting so you can respond to God's giving. People who don't know God and the way he works fuss over these things, but you know both God and how he works. Steep yourself in God-reality, God-initiative, God-provisions. You'll find all your everyday human concerns will be met. Don't be afraid of missing out. You're my dearest friends! The Father wants to give you the very kingdom itself." (Luke 12:29–32 MSG)

It's not just your everyday human concerns that will be met. It's also your everyday parental concerns. The Father—your Father—wants to give you the very kingdom itself. He wants to give it to your child too. He wants to pull out all the stops to give you both more good than you can imagine. That's the kind of love He lavishes on you.

So, what is your response? Knowing the depth of His love for you and for your child. You can trust. You can be grateful. You can immerse yourself in prayer, in the Word, and in community because you have been given so very much.

How would your parenting look different if you really trusted God?

We have a friend who has a blackboard in her kitchen. On it are the words "Mostly what God does is love you," taken from Ephesians 5 in *The Message*. As her teenage children walk in and out of the kitchen, twenty-seven times a day, they are reminded. She's not stopping them to pray over them. She's not calling them into the family room for a devotional, although she could do any of those things. But in her discerning heart, she senses they are at an age where quiet reminders speak the loudest.

Another mom we know prays the same prayer with her son every morning. He started kindergarten this year and he cries most mornings before school. He's afraid, and his fear beckons her to follow. But she trusts instead. She trusts and prays, with her son, every morning this simple prayer: "Good morning, Lord. This is Your day. I am your child. Show me the way."

You may not feel like you're a very spiritual parent. If you were to ask these moms, they would say that they don't either. But they need Jesus. They need Him to meet them when they get angry with their children, forget to pray, forget to love in the way He has called them to. They are growing up in Christ. And they are already grown up enough to know that needing Him is plenty. We need. He gives. We get to respond out of all He

has lavished upon us. You can't be Jesus, but you can need Him
severely, and your children get to stand back and watch this
glorious and merciful Savior work. It's pretty simple, after all.

Trust and obey, for there's no other way
To be happy in Jesus, but to trust and obey.

Not a shadow can rise, not a cloud in the skies,
But His smile quickly drives it away;
Not a doubt or a fear, not a sigh or a tear,
Can abide while we trust and obey.

JOHN H. SAMMIS, 1887

10.

Being a Merciful Parent

—with David

I HAD JUST GOTTEN BACK IN TOWN FROM SPEAK-
ing in Oklahoma. While away, my wife called to say she got an
e-mail from one of our son's teachers, requesting to speak with
her. Have you ever noticed that when teachers call or e-mail, it's
rarely ever good news?

I can't remember a time of getting a call to say, "I just wanted
you to know that your child is on target academically, a delight
to have as a student, a real leader in the classroom. This is just a
call to encourage you as a parent."

So, I braced myself for the news and whatever cleanup might
be required on the other side of my trip. Turns out, it was a somewhat minor offense in the big scheme of things. My son finished
a test early and was bored waiting on his classmates to finish, so

he decided to entertain himself by throwing an eraser at a friend while the teacher's back was turned to the class. The evidence surfaced when she turned around to find the class laughing, an eraser on the floor, and his buddy rubbing the back of his head.

I don't think we would've gotten a call had this been the only offense. Strike two came when she asked who threw the eraser and no one confessed. She did a bit of investigating, questioned different individuals, and when asked if my son threw the eraser, he calmly said he didn't.

That's when it became a big deal. He lied. He didn't *just* lie; he looked her right in the eyes and said, "I didn't do it."

The first offense is what I call stupid. Boys are prone to a lot of stupid, in my opinion. *A lot* of stupid. I could tell you stories of boy stupid that would make your head spin around sideways—shooting rocks from slingshots at car windows; hiding alcohol in the garage and thinking their dad won't find it; painting on lockers in a newly renovated school building; making out with a girl in the baseball coach's office; speeding and chasing a school bus; and the list goes on and on. A lot of stupid is revealed in the ER, the principal's office, or the back of a police car.

My friend Katherine once said, "Stupid has consequences." I'm a firm believer in stupid having consequences. I know parents who say things like, "He didn't really mean to," or "He just wasn't thinking." These words seem to assume he should be let off the hook since he obviously wasn't thinking clearly or was "just being a boy."

I wasn't thinking two weeks ago when I was driving forty-two in a thirty-mile-per-hour zone. I was being stupid, and I'll remember that when I go to traffic school next month. Stupid has consequences.

So, back to my son, he was having a stupid moment. He is a

bright, creative kid and could have grabbed a copy of the paper-back in his backpack to read if he was bored. He's also smart enough to know that lying is considered a federal offense at his school and that his teacher is smart enough to figure out what went down when her back was turned. She knows all she has to do is ask a girl in the class, because girls will spill the beans. Furthermore, he's been around long enough to know that his mother and I support his teacher, think she's an all-star, and aren't the kind of parents to come running to school to get him off the hook.

That's something else worth noting with boys: despite what they know, it often flies right out of their heads and into the stratosphere somewhere. Anytime I speak on boys, I always begin with some education on the boy brain. The boy brain is a strange, mysterious, fascinating place to visit. I talk about a boy's neurochemistry and how he's wired for activity and movement. I speak of how girls tend to think first and act second, a very logical series of events. Boys, on the other hand, tend to act first and then think, *I wonder if that was a good idea or not.*

My smart, creative son was obviously having an act-first, think-second kind of moment. He is now facing a stupid-has-consequences moment.

My wife got the call; his teacher reported the stupid and informed us of her plan of action. It involved missing recess, the call home, some research on lying, and an apology letter to his friend.

Because I was out of town, we decided my wife would address it that day after school and I'd talk with him upon my return to let him know we were all on the same page, and that I support his teacher and his mom.

He had a birthday party to attend that afternoon at this crazy-cool sports facility in town, so we decided he would stay home from that and do his research, write his letter, and feel some of the gravity of this episode. Needless to say, this announcement was the worst news he'd received in a while.

In the end, we were hoping for a connecting of the dots from him. We wanted to send a strong message that he's a bright, resourceful, creative kid who chose to be lazy and foolish in that moment. His decision had a price tag attached to it. More than the eraser, our bigger concern resided with his looking his teacher in the face and lying to her. We wanted to send a *strong* message that lying will never work well for him.

When I checked in with him upon my return, I simply wanted to reassure him that he is loved enough to be found out. What a gift that is! He can't fully wrap his young mind around that right now, but he will understand more someday. I remain grateful that I'm loved enough by a God who, in His mercy, allows me to be found out. He consistently, gently, sometimes painfully, continues to expose my sin and all the crud that encircles my heart. It's a gift.

The longer I live this truth as an adult, and the longer I parent my three children through this journey, I know that being "found out" sometimes happens immediately upon sinning, sometimes shortly after, and sometimes down the road.

The other process that takes place, that is so familiar to me, is this gentle work of the Holy Spirit, where I experience guilt and shame in the face of my own stupid—that nudging, relentless, uneasy feeling that accompanies the dishonest, destructive, deceitful decisions I make that lay hidden. I have lived with this discomfort while waiting to be "found out."

I talked with my son about that nudging, relentless, uneasy feeling he felt while looking at his teacher and being dishonest with her, and how he felt it as he walked away from her back to his desk. I told him the discomfort is a gift from the Holy Spirit . . . evidence of a love that will not let him go. I described it as mercy, because I believe it is.

Learning Through Observation

In my household we talk a lot about how much there is to be learned through observation. Maybe it's looking back on a mistake we've made and considering how we could have done something differently. Sometimes learning through observation comes when we watch the decisions that friends make that we'd want to duplicate and those we'd prefer not to repeat.

My daughter recently commented about a girlfriend of hers who asks great initiating questions. This friend has a remarkable way of making people feel that she is interested in who they are in her everyday conversations. Questions like, "When was the birthday when you felt the most celebrated?" or "What makes it feel like summer vacation for you?" This friend is engaging, warm, interested, and gifted with a remarkable ability to make you feel like a genuine priority.

My boys recently spent time with a friend who has a habit of asking for a lot. They observed that he walks into a gas station or drugstore making requests for a purchase as he crosses the threshold of the door. We all reflected on our tendency toward entitlement and a habit of confusing our needs and our wants. It was a simple observation, a mental note of sorts that allows us to pay attention to the way the decisions we make affect the people around us.

We make these observations in real time with ourselves, with the people around us, and with characters in films and books we love. Every day I learn so much through the parents I sit with in my office. I certainly hear stories that remind me of decisions I'd rather not duplicate, but it's just as common to hear parents share stories that inspire and stir me in my own parenting.

Recently, a mom shared a story of finding out, through a friend/neighbor, that her son had experimented with alcohol after a game and then drove home with another adolescent in the car. The story came to light when the friend called and noticed the boy driving recklessly near the entrance of their neighborhood. The mom approached her son at breakfast the next morning (once he was sober, because it does little good to confront or lecture an intoxicated adolescent). She wisely didn't ask, "Were you drinking last night?" She knew that question might lead to the same answer my son gave when confronted about the flying eraser.

She simply said, "I got a call from a concerned person who witnessed you driving recklessly last night. Before you ask, it doesn't matter who it was; it matters that you drank, you aren't of age, and you got behind the wheel of a car. I could tell you'd just used mouthwash when you walked in and hugged me good night. After breakfast, you'll bring me your car keys, and your car will sit in the driveway until your father gets back in town and we have a chance to talk about how long you are grounded."

The boy knew he was caught. She didn't set him up to lie, and he knew this was an opportunity to step into the truth. His mom continued by saying, "You betrayed our trust, you put your-self and anyone on the road last night in danger, and you created liability for your father and me. You won't drive again until you rebuild that trust. We'll talk about what that looks like."

She finished by saying, "More than anything, I'm glad some-one saw you. Since you were young, I've prayed that you would be found out. No matter how much heartache that brings in your life, I want you to live a clean life. A life that reflects who I believe God made you to be."

She grabbed his hand, smiled through watery eyes, and left the table. She left him to sit with the beautiful reminder that her highest priority in life is not his happiness, but his health—his physical, emotional, and spiritual health.

Mercy in Action

Another father who taught me something through observation is the dad of a young man whose story I first read a long time ago. A young man came to his father and asked for access to his inheritance. We don't have evidence within this story that the young fella had a strong plan or strategy. He launched out into the world, spending his wealth in wild living. He sounds like a high percentage of young men I work with who head off to a big SEC school with the money their parents have saved for college.

According to the Scripture, we're told this young man "came to his senses" when dining with pigs. This was his connecting-of-the-dots moment; he somehow realized he had a great gig back home and should consider heading back.

He headed home, and while he was a long way off, his

father saw him and his heart was moved at the sight of this broken boy. The father's response is as powerful a picture of mercy as any I know. The only thing the father knew to do was run to him and embrace him. There is so much forgiveness in his response.

He didn't meet the boy with folded arms, or an "I told you so," or "Look who is home without any money." There is no judgment, no condemnation, no criticism.

Sissy and I teach a class called Life After High School. The class is for parents of junior and seniors, and it's designed to talk about preparing kids to leave home and transition into the next stage of young adulthood. During one part of the class, we talk about what happens if you find yourself parenting a child who needs to come home for one reason or another. I encourage parents to reread this story as a reminder of many things.

One is the reminder that there is no lecture involved. This wise father didn't diminish the power of the experience by adding a lecture to the mix. He saw evidence that this boy had connected the dots through failing.

I often laugh with parents in asking, "Aren't you the least bit curious about what was going on for the mom in this story? Can you imagine how hard it was for her to bite her tongue (or for the dad to silence her)? What do you think was going on in her mind while the father was handing the cash over to the boy? Thoughts like, *Are you out of your mind giving this much money to an adolescent?* Or what was she tempted to say at the sight of him walking toward the house? Was her heart moved in the same way or did she consider throttling him?"

Whatever was going on for the both of them, it's another picture of parenting out of love, not fear.

Modeling Forgiveness

As much as the father extended mercy and forgiveness to this young man, he modeled it as well. Kids learn more through observation than information. This boy had wasted all of his father's money. He hadn't invested it wisely, he didn't have a formal education to show for it, and the money was simply gone. He didn't deserve the mercy extended to him. His father demonstrated something powerful in this exchange.

I believe extending mercy is also a means of teaching empathy. My friend Julie is a professor at a university. She happens to also be an amazing artist. She created a painting that hangs in her home with a quote by Plato that reads, "Be kind, for everyone you meet is fighting a hard battle."

I want my kids to grow into an understanding that everyone they meet is fighting some kind of battle. We could all use some kindness and mercy. The more we extend this to our children and to people around us, the more familiar it feels to our kids.

Equally important is that they see us extend grace and forgiveness to ourselves. Moms, you, in particular, expect a lot of yourself and have a hard time forgiving yourself. Never lose sight of the reality that your daughters are watching closely and learning how a woman handles failure, disappointment, and adversity, among other things. Dads, our sons are tuned into the same channel. We are the first place they learn how a man navigates these same experiences. Do they see a guy who shuts down, goes off the deep end, or spews emotion all over his family? It's vital that kids see us being kind to ourselves (and others) and willing to forgive (ourselves and others) when we blow it.

What battle might your son/daughter be fighting right now?

What battle are you currently fighting as a parent?

Leaving the Past

It's not uncommon to sit in a parent consultation and hear one or both parents say, "We should have come in months [or years] ago." I'm quick to respond to that statement by saying, "Well, I'm grateful you are here now." Sometimes we have trouble letting go of the "I should have" moments.

Letting go of the things we wish we'd done opens up more space to focus on the things we can do now. Regret is a powerful force. It takes up a lot of emotional space and doesn't leave much room for intentionality or creativity. We aren't talking about forgetting the past or acting as if it didn't take place. Those are two different forms of denial. We are recommending learning from the past and taking that knowledge into the present and the future.

An example of this would be the mom whose son was drinking and driving, or the father of the prodigal son. That mom could have lived in the question of "How did I miss that he was drinking?" or "I shouldn't have let him spend so much time with that particular friend." The father of the prodigal could have gotten buried in, "What if I had not given him access to that much money to blow?"

At some point, the mom will need to give driving privileges back to the son, and the father will need to trust his son with money again. It wouldn't help either of these boys to never have access to freedom or finances again. They need both to adequately prepare them for adulthood.

Both parents will look for the right moment to give back a little freedom and responsibility, and to see how that much is handled. If handled responsibly, then give a little bit more. And then a little bit more.

If (or maybe when) both of these boys blow it again, you repeat the process and wait for the connecting-the-dots moments. Some kids are slower to come into these moments than others. The hit-and-miss can be difficult, if not downright agonizing, to watch at times.

Reflect for a moment on any evidence of regret or resentment, a place where you have avoided extending forgiveness to yourself or your child that needs attention.

Avoiding a Lecture

As we wait on our kids to make these connections, and for the long, slow process of maturity to take place, it's important to pay attention to expectations and communication. There are times when, without intending to do so, we set our kids up for failure.

I'm at Fido, my favorite Nashville breakfast spot, seated across from a couple with a young boy who looks to be about eighteen months old. He is squirmy, active, and moving all over the place. If his parents turn their heads for a moment, he shimmies his way out of the chair and onto the floor, testing his newest escape plan. His parents are trying desperately to enjoy the warm breakfast in front of them. You can tell they worked hard to make this morning happen. They both have wet hair, indicating a shower (or spit bath); the diaper bag looks packed; the fancy stroller is stocked with toys and objects to distract him while they make an attempt at eating.

It's not working. They've now strapped him in the chair and he's bowed backward, throwing silverware against the wall.

This young boy is like a puppy. He wants to move and play, to wreak havoc on this place. He cannot sit still to save his life. I should shut my laptop and offer to chase him around the coffee-house while they eat. This scene is dangerously familiar to me. I can remember "attempting" to eat out with my twin sons when they were this age. It's rigged to fail.

Restaurants should just hang a sign on the door that says . . .

NO SMOKING

NO PETS

NO BOYS UNDER THE AGE OF FIVE

They'd be doing us all a favor. It rarely ever works. To expect this young boy to sit quietly and enjoy breakfast is like asking me to walk in Ben & Jerry's and just watch, not ordering a thing. It's not going to happen.

A more realistic expectation might have been for the family to pack the car, call in the order, swing by to pick it up, and enjoy it outdoors at a park while Moving Marcus was on the loose. He could roam while his parents enjoyed their breakfast and watched.

Parents often ask my thoughts on coed sleepovers. Yes, you read that correctly, coed sleepovers for high school–aged kids. It's become a popular thing. In my opinion, it's even more foolish than taking a toddler boy to a restaurant. I usually respond to that question with a question of my own. Something like, "What are you hoping the outcome will be?" Or "Help me understand your objective." I avoid saying things like, "Are you on crack?"

Again, be realistic in setting expectations. If you were an advocate for teen pregnancy, then coed sleepovers would make sense. Otherwise, putting testosterone-filled, hormonally charged, regulation-deficient adolescent boys in the same space with adolescent girls overnight would make as much sense as building a bonfire in your living room and hosing it with gasoline.

Another scenario is the question of serving alcohol to teens at a party in your home as long as you take their keys, believing that you are preparing them for adulthood and not breaking the law. No matter how you spin it, serving alcohol to minors is against the law. And expecting them to act responsibly while under the influence is foolish.

The toddler brain is only capable of certain functions. The adolescent brain has limitations as well. We have to set *realistic expectations* to match their *developmental process*.

When we do set realistic expectations and they blow it, which they will certainly do in their process of growing up, this is the moment for discipline and consequences. Here's another moment where we strongly recommend the Parenting with Love and Logic series. It covers kids from six months through adolescence. Run, don't walk, to your nearest bookstore or library.

The great folks at Love and Logic talk repeatedly about responding with empathy when our kids blow it. We don't have to yell, scream, or go off the deep end. We simply respond lovingly with empathy and consequences. Remember, we are providing connecting-of-the-dots moments and waiting to see some evidence that this is happening.

A great example of these ideas tied together came from a

wise mom who shared this story with me in a parent consultation. Her son, like most adolescent boys I know, couldn't get to his sixteenth birthday fast enough. As the date approached, he counted down with much anticipation. She checked him out of school on the actual day to get his license and to go to lunch to celebrate this milestone in his life. He navigated the first months of having his license with success and then (like many adolescent boys I know) began experimenting a bit with his new freedom. Every time he violated the contract they had created, they limited his freedoms, put some parameters around the freedom, and then gave him an opportunity to earn back some trust.

On one occasion, he left the house, announcing he was headed to basketball practice and would be home afterward. His mom remembered thinking he seemed a bit *too* enthusiastic about practice on this particular day. The son was well aware that a part of his consequence for violating trust during his last escapade involved his parents adding the GPS component to his cell phone. He must have forgotten that part of the conversation (remember how information flies out of their heads and into the stratosphere), because he headed straight for stupid.

His mother logged on to the home computer thirty minutes after his departure, which would have been plenty of time for him to arrive safely at the school gym for practice. The tracking device identified his car in a remote parking lot not far from their home, but nowhere near his school. His mother grabbed her keys and headed toward the destination. She parked her car a distance from his location and began walking toward his car.

As she approached the vehicle, she could see there were two people in the front seat, though their heads were smashed together, making it look like one. As she got closer, it became obvious that it was his girlfriend. He'd managed to pick her up on the way to "practice," though he was engaged in a different kind of practice at this time.

His mother walked to his side of the car and tapped on the window. She asked the question, "How's practice?"

The boy turned in shock and began adjusting his shorts, just as his girlfriend began immediately buttoning her shirt.

The mom gave them a moment to collect themselves and then said to her son, "Follow me." She then motioned to the young lady to walk with her toward her vehicle.

She rode in silence with his teary girlfriend back to her home. They parked in her driveway and exited the vehicles. The mom then said to her son, "Let's apologize." They knocked on the door, and her father answered, looking confused at finding his teary daughter, her deer-in-the-headlights boyfriend, and his mother standing on their doorstep.

This mom reported to me what it was like to watch her son sit in front of this girl's father, admit to deceiving him by saying he was taking his daughter to get dinner when his intention was to park and make out in the car. He had to sit in the humiliation, the being found out, awaiting this father's response to his decision.

I applauded the mom for creating this great connecting-the-dots moment, and for how little she said throughout and following the exchange. Did you note how few words she spoke throughout the incident?

"How's practice?"

"Follow me."

"Let's apologize."

Those six powerful words were more than enough. She could have so easily flooded him with questions or emotions. She could've verbally assaulted the boy out of her own frustration, disappointment, anger, and fear. Rather than lecturing, she did a beautiful job of allowing the experience to be the teacher.

Evidently the girl's father spoke strongly to the boy about being lied to. He reminded the boy that he had allowed him to leave the house with one of his greatest treasures, told him he'd lost permission to see her outside of their home, but ended by saying, "We acknowledge your apology, and we forgive you."

This boy experienced consequences while also being extended mercy, a mercy that he had not earned or deserved.

Undeserved Favor

We are given so many opportunities in parenting. I opened the book with Dan Allender's words on parenting as an opportunity to grow up, to be changed, and to be transformed. Elizabeth Stone said, "Making the decision to have a child is momentous. It is to decide forever to have your heart go walking around outside your body."[1] I once heard Anne Lamott comment that parenting is an opportunity to let go and stop leaving such deep claw marks.

We'd say it's all of the above. It's also an opportunity to live out this truth in front of our kids. "When the kindness and love of God our Savior appeared, he saved us, not because of righteous things we had done, but because of his mercy" (Titus 3:4–5 NIV). We're given so many opportunities to put feet to that truth in parenting, to simply love our kids where they are. We're

invited to love them not for what they do, not for how they perform academically or athletically, not for how well they behave
or what choices they make, but simply for who they are. That's
the kind of love and kindness that has been extended to us. We
weren't saved because of outstanding, worthy choices we'd made
or how we performed as people. In fact, we got the opposite of
what we really deserved. We were saved because of His mercy.

How could you make that truth more real to your kids?

*Write a note and put it under their pillows tonight. Send them
each an e-mail where you just name what you love, value, and
respect in them. Read it out loud again to them before they go
to bed.*

Years ago, some friends of mine adopted a little boy from
Africa. They took the long, slow journey so many parents take in
pursuing adoption—the mounds of paperwork, the home visits,
the financial burden of the process, the traveling overseas, the
waiting, and the not knowing. The final chapter involved standing outside an orphanage on the other side of the world and
laying eyes on this little boy they'd only seen in photographs for
the first time. They chronicled their journey through pictures
and video they shared with family and friends. You can see his
face when being held by his father for the first time, his big sister
reaching for him at the airport, and his grandparents holding
him and weeping uncontrollably.

One of my favorite moments is when they arrived at their
home after days of traveling across the globe and were welcomed
at the airport. They pulled into their driveway late that night

with this sleepy child to find friends lining the sidewalk to their front door, holding candles and singing hymns. As they exited the car and walked this boy to the steps of his forever home, he was surrounded by all these people who loved him without yet knowing him, and had prayed him to this place. They softly, gently sang this great truth over his little life.

Had my friends not taken the long, slow journey of adoption, who knows how this boy's life would have played out. I don't know how long he would've lived, or who would have cared for him if he did. I don't know what he would have done to survive his past circumstances.

What I do know is that he was adopted into a family with a mom and dad who love him, a big brother and sister who can't take their hands off him, and grandparents and community surrounding him. He has access to all the basics of life—food, shelter, and a chance to grow and thrive—that weren't afforded to him in the first months of his life. He was saved by love, literally.

So was I. I didn't experience adoption in the same way, but I am a beneficiary of a spiritual adoption. I have the same thread of undeserved favor as a part of my story. That story belongs to my children as well. I have an obligation to help them grow up with some understanding of the kind of mercy that has been extended to them, as I continue embracing that truth for myself. That's being a merciful parent.

11.

Being a Hopeful Parent

—with Sissy

"SAME." THE WORD WAS SAID QUIETLY ACROSS the table. "SAME," this time with a little more volume. "Same." "Same." "Same." Over and over again.

It was a Tuesday night in early fall. I was sitting outside a restaurant, eating dinner with a group of high school girls, which, in my world, means I was leading a group counseling session for Daystar. One by one, these girls talked about how they were struggling . . . friends, boys, families. As each girl expressed her heart, someone else in the group quietly (or loudly) remarked, "Same."

My hope is that this chapter brings about the same response from you, as a parent. Being a hopeful parent can be incredibly difficult at times. Every parent loses hope. If you haven't yet, which would most likely mean that you're reading this in the hospital with your newborn, you will soon. It could be the first night, or more likely the twenty-seventh night of no sleep and not enough naps between sunup and sundown. (Some of you are saying, "Same" right now.) It could be that your daughter comes down with RSV, or some other frightening illness, at just a few months of age. (A few more "same's.") Maybe your three-year-old son rages anytime you tell him no. Your twelve-year-old daughter isn't invited to yet another birthday party. Your sixteen-year-old son tried marijuana for the first time. "Same." "Same." "Same." He hurts. She hurts. You hurt. And you lose hope.

I recently met with one such hopeless parent. Her fourth-grade daughter was one of many I've seen in my office recently struggling with anxiety. We'll call her Allie. On the outside, Allie was bubbly, bright, and energetic. On the inside, she was a nervous wreck. She worried about everything and could fall apart or, even more likely, become enraged at any moment the worry struck. She thought that if her mom was late picking her up from school, she'd died in a car accident. If her dad was five minutes late taking her to school, she would fail the fourth grade. Her mom was not just sad for Allie but weary from her daughter's constant barrage of questions and fears. Because of Allie's pain and struggle, her mom was losing hope.

One day, in my office, Allie literally came undone over the fact that her mom went to McDonald's to get a Diet Coke every day before she picked her up from school. "None of the other mothers drive through McDonald's every day. They just come and pick their daughters up with a snack and a drink. I DON'T UNDERSTAND WHY YOU HAVE TO GO TO McDONALD'S!" In only a few moments, Allie's bubbly exterior had disintegrated into a teary rage.

I knew that to really help Allie work through her anxiety,

we had to get to the root of what was behind it. We had to find out what it was about her mom's daily McDonald's drive that touched on Allie's fear. After a long discussion, Allie was finally able to verbalize to her mom, "I'm afraid that since you're driving through McDonald's, you don't care about our nutrition any longer. You're going to let our whole family get fat and die."

Quite a jump from a daily Diet Coke to death by lack of nutrition. But that was little Allie's logic. Or at least it was her brain's logic when she hit those anxious places.

As a parent, your brain can do the same thing. It can, obviously, when you worry. But it also can when you start to lose hope. When your child struggles, talks back, is ill, or any number of daily situations when raising a child, logic goes out the window. You get frustrated. Upset. Sad. And then you panic. "My child will never . . ."; you can fill in the blank. You start to lose sight of the truths you know about your child, yourself, and even God. Instead of operating out of those truths, you operate on the basis of a lie.

In this chapter, we're going to explore six of the most common lies hopeless parents say to themselves. We're going to get to the root of these lies, just as I did with Allie's nutritional fears. And then we're going to explore the truths that can not only battle each particular lie, but that can free you to be the hopeful parent God has called you to be.

Lie #1: Everyone else has perfect
_____.

You get to fill in the blank on this one. Actually, you probably already have. I think that, as parents, this one starts early.

"Everyone else's child is crawling . . . or walking . . . or speaking in complete sentences."

I recently met with a group of parents of school-age and adolescent children. I had them fill in their own blanks. These were just a few . . .

"Everyone else's child can read."

"Everyone else's child passed their driver's permit exam the *first* time."

"Everyone else's child is doing well in school."

"Everyone else's child makes friends easily."

"Everyone else seems like a smarter parent than I am."

"Everyone else gets along with their kid."

Write three statements you say to yourself that start with, "Everyone else _____."

The very important truth behind all of these lies is:

Truth #1: Every child and every family struggles.

Some just hide it better than others.

A favorite author of all three of us, Anne Lamott, described a fight she had with her teenage son in her book *Plan B*. She explained how she handled the fight and how she battles her own lies she tells herself as a mom:

> The usual things helped: some distance, prayer, chocolate. Talking to the parents of older kids was helpful for me, since parents of kids the same ages as yours won't admit how horrible their children are.[1]

Because we're counselors, parents typically admit it to us . . . in our offices, that is. But there are times when I'll walk a parent to the lobby of Daystar, and she or he is shocked to see someone he or she knows waiting for his/her own counseling appointment. I can't count the times neighbors or coworkers, community group members or even teachers and students have accidentally and somewhat awkwardly greeted each other in our lobby. In reality, it shouldn't be awkward. Daystar currently serves more than nine hundred families in the middle Tennessee community. That's a lot of people. And we're just one of many counseling offices in one city in one country. People are hurting. Children are struggling. Parents are lost—and have lost hope. We are a broken people. And that brokenness pervades *all* of our families.

Lie #2: My kids don't like me or listen to me.

Preschool Parenting Spoiler Alert: This lie is particularly pointed toward parents of preteens and teenagers.

It's always interesting to speak to parents of preschoolers. There are several differences in a crowd of preschool parents versus parents of teens. The parents of younger children have a little more hope in their faces, as well as a little more confidence. Most look as if they feel relatively in control. They have stories about the "cute" things their children do. They laugh when David talks about boys putting marbles up their noses and get teary when I talk about a dad delighting in his young daughter.

But then, we introduce the topic of teenagers. We talk about normal development for a teen . . . how they all get sulky, roll their eyes, use one-word answers. (You're loudly shouting "Same!" at this point if you have a teenager at home.) Narcissism is actually the word we use most often to describe these awkward adolescents. And for those confident, hopeful preschool parents to hear that their children *will* be embarrassed by them and push them away strikes terror into their hearts. You can see it in their wide eyes and hear it in the comments afterward, such as, "Surely, my daughter won't . . ." or "Does every teenage boy really . . . ?"

But, if you're living with a child between the ages of eleven and eighteen, you know what it feels like not to be heard, and even not to be liked from time to time. (Actually, we're having more and more parents tell us their children are showing signs of teenagedom in their grade-school years.)

You try to talk to your son about an e-mail you received from his teacher, and he quickly picks up his phone and starts texting. You tell your daughter how important it is that she be kind and speak to your family at Thanksgiving. She says, *"Dad, I know,"* with as much disdain as her fourteen-year-old face can communicate. Your teens either cut you off mid-sentence or their eyes glaze over three minutes into a conversation.

You don't feel heard and you often don't feel liked. Your son breezes past you with, "Mom, I've got homework," when you try to ask him about his day. You invite your daughter to dinner and she has "too much to do." You aren't thanked, aren't really spoken to or even looked at many times, and certainly aren't enjoyed.

The truth we would say is this:

Truth #2, Part A: They see and hear
far more than you can imagine.

Melissa tells a story about a meeting she had with a group of parents whose children had all become adults. She asked the question, "What do you wish you had known when your children were younger?" One dad said, "I wish I had known how much impact I had. I just had no idea."

You have impact. They hear you. And in their teenage years as well, they're watching you more than you know. They listen to the words you speak and then watch your actions for the ways you live out those words.

I had an interesting session just last week with a teenage mother and daughter; it was one that reflects a lot of what I think happens in this communication breakdown between parents and teens.

Mom wanted Courtney to spend more time with the family. So, she started telling her how important it was. Three words in, Courtney did the whole stare-off-into-space thing. So, her mom re-explained it a different way. And then another and another and another. Courtney never really responded, so finally her mom moved on to the next point, which was that her sister thought she was being rude at home. Courtney shrank farther into the couch, and her mom just kept going.

After her mom left, I said, "You just don't really want to be parented, do you?" to fifteen-year-old Courtney. She smiled sheepishly and said, "Not really. But my mom does give pretty good advice." Her mom never would have known that by Courtney's responses—or lack thereof.

You have no idea the impact you have. And often, since you

don't see it in her eyes, and since she doesn't say, "Mom, thanks for the great advice," you keep going.

People who talk about parenting, including us, often say how important it is to choose your battles with teenagers. Undoubtedly, it is. But it is equally important that you choose your words. She hears you. He hears you. But he probably stops listening after the first paragraph. So, make your words count. Engage him in the conversation. Ask him what he thinks. Ask her how she feels about a situation. And trust that you have impact, even if it doesn't register on his or her teenage face.

Truth #2, Part B: You're the parent. It matters more that your child respect you than like you.

There has been a lot of talk about "buddy parenting" in the past few years. It's often a response to the authoritarian parenting that many of our generation grew up with. It makes sense that you want your children to feel connected and close to you, in a way that maybe you didn't to your mom or dad. But in their teenage years, even if they feel close to you, they're probably not going to act like it. I remember a seventh grader telling me she wasn't close to her mom anymore because she was "a teenager and wasn't supposed to be."

Your teenagers have plenty of buddies. But they only have one set of parents. When you try to "buddy parent," you lose the respect of your child and you often set him or her up to feel inse- cure. As a matter of fact, I believe that two of the best builders for self-esteem in kids are for them to feel safe and to feel enjoyed. We've already addressed the enjoyment part, and what helps them feel safe is when they know that you are stronger than they are.

When your children feel like the most powerful member of your family, they feel insecure. It's too much. Several years ago, a teenage girl told me she started talking back to her mom just to get her mom to give her consequences. "I really want to be grounded. It's like I just need to know that when I push her, she won't fall down. I want to know that she's the parent and that she's stronger."

In the absence of a strong parent, kids will often either push you to see your strength or feel that they have to rise to the occasion themselves. They become adultified children, feeling as if their job is to take care of you, since you don't seem strong enough to take care of them. Both situations can create resentment and insecurity on the part of your child.

Don't be afraid to be the parent. Your teenager's like or dislike of you is more about his or her adolescent angst than it is about your style of parenting. Your teens will come back around as they grow up, and they'll respect you more for being the steady, strong parent God has made you to be. You'll probably respect yourself a little more along the way too.

Lie #3: I am all alone.

You may be a single parent. You may have lost your spouse to cancer, an accident, or some other tragedy. You are the mom and the dad to your child and feel overwhelmed on your best days . . . and lost and hopeless on your worst.

You may be divorced with a co-parent who doesn't care a thing about co-parenting. You and your son haven't heard from him in years. It would be nice to share visitation and have at least one night alone every so often. Or even to have someone else who cares about the report cards and doctor's visits. But you don't. And you feel alone.

You may "co-parent" with Mickey Mouse. She or he is the quintessential fun parent—Disneyland in a box. Every time the kids go to his house, it's all fun, all the time. Your ex cares more about the next high-dollar, fun activity than about homework or cell phone limits. You can't keep up with the costs and know your children need boundaries that the other parent isn't offering. You feel frustrated and isolated.

It could even be that you live in the same home with your child's other parent. You eat meals together—most of the time. You go to his or her sporting events and school programs together. But you just can't get on the same page. He never backs you up with discipline. She is so critical of the children that it feels as if you're doing more damage control than parenting. You are living together but parenting alone.

Truth #3: You don't have to be. You and your child need other voices.

In any of the above situations, you need support. You need what we refer to as "other voices." As a matter of fact, we tell Daystar parents that we're not really saying anything different to their children than they are. We're just a new voice. Often they'll hear us in a different way. You need those other voices. You can't do it alone and don't have to.

It is of utmost importance, for your well-being and that of your child, that you have support. Your church can provide that kind of environment for both of you. There is no shame in asking for help. Go to the children's minister and ask what programs your child could become involved in. Is there any type of mentoring program for men or women—whichever parent is missing in the life of your child? Could your kids join a small group where they will meet kids from all type of homes, some similar to yours? Could the youth minister or a trusted volunteer invest specifically in your son's or daughter's life? Take him to lunch? Have coffee with her?

If, for some reason, your church is not set up to provide this, what about his or her school? Is there a teacher or coach you trust? A guidance counselor that could start a small group or spend some one-on-one time with your son or daughter? Is there a Big Brother/Big Sister program in your community or some other type of mentoring organization? Our friends at Google can help you find lots of programs as well, but make sure to get references and to research anyone or any place with which your child is involved.

It may even be that counseling would be helpful for your child, or for you. For years, I had a single mom who brought her children and would come in, at times, just for herself. "We've hit this snag with school [or with friends, or the opposite sex] and I'm not sure what to do. I need another parent, and you're it today." At Daystar, we have kids who come regularly through a crisis. And then we have kids who come once a month or even just periodically when issues arise, because their parents want another voice for their children and themselves. Obviously, counseling can be expensive. But there are great resources out there that offer sliding scales based on your ability to pay and/or insurance reimbursement. Again, your church can help you find those. The American Association of Christian Counselors also has a website with lots of resources at www.aacc.net.

One of my favorite stories in the Bible is in Exodus 17. It's when Moses and the Israelites were fighting the Amalekites. Moses stood on a hill overlooking the battle with the staff of God in his hands. Whenever he held up his arms, the Israelites would be winning. As soon as he lowered his arms, they would lose. Obviously, Moses could not hold his arms up for hours on end, so his friends Aaron and Hur sat him down on a stone and stood on either side of him, holding up his arms so that the Israelites would win the battle.

Parenting will be one of the biggest battles you will ever face. Just as we're talking about in this chapter, you'll lose hope. Your arms will drop. You cannot fight this battle alone. Pray that God would lead you to the right arm-raising resources. Talk to friends. Again, don't be afraid to ask for help. God calls us to live in community, and that community exists to make sure none of us are alone.

Lie #4: Nothing works.

If I had a nickel, as they say . . .

I have had some semblance of the same conversation countless times over the years.

"I would suggest time-out, with increasing increments of time based on his response," I say.

"We've tried it. It doesn't work for him," they say.

"Why don't you try taking away her cell phone for the night?" I say.

"Tried it. She doesn't care," they say.

"One thing we suggest is having your son run laps around

the house. You can increase the amount of laps if he continues the behavior. It usually runs out his negative energy, and then he'll often talk about whatever it is that's going on," I say.

"We've already done that. It didn't help," they say.

On and on, *ad nauseum*, and much to my consternation. As a counselor, I get to a point at which I'm out of ideas. The parents feel as if they are as well. But over the years, I have learned a truth that I think is particularly vital for the parents who feel as though nothing works.

Truth #4: Consistency works.
And so does love and logic.

In my experience, the parents who feel that nothing helps are often buffet-table types of parents. They circle around the buffet, sampling a little of this and a little of that, trying to find the perfect consequence. They felt guilty about spanking after the first time, so they never did that again. Time-outs didn't seem to make much difference after a week, so they needed a new option. When they told him he had to clean his sister's room after hitting her, it just seemed to make him treat her worse. There are as many reasons the consequences don't work as there are consequences to sample. There is no perfect consequence. It's the consistency that matters more. We've already spoken to this in our chapter on consistency, but it is important enough that it bears reinforcement.

At an early age, kids are onto us adults. I have children of all ages say to me, behind closed doors, "My mom and dad yell, but they don't do anything about it." Or, "I know if I act like it doesn't bother me, they won't do it again." Or even, "My parents give me consequences all the time but never follow through."

No matter how old your children are as you're reading this, they know how to read you. They know that if they act as if taking away the television doesn't matter, next time you'll try to take away something else. And then they get to watch TV. They know how to bluff and how to get out of things, if you'll let them out. Consistency works.

Choose a type of consequence. If you come up with a chart where they get checks every time they remember to clean their rooms, help with their chores, and have their homework signed, stick with the chart. Use it for a good month or two before you give up on it. If you tell your daughter you're going to take away her cell phone every time she's disrespectful, take it away. She will test you to see if you're serious. She wants her cell phone, even if she acts as though she doesn't care. And increase the consequence if the behavior continues. She lost a Friday night activity because she lied. If she lies again, she needs to lose Saturday night as well.

In terms of consequence ideas, we would again defer to our favorite series of books on discipline, which is called the Love and Logic series. There is *Love and Logic Magic for Early Childhood*, *Parenting with Love and Logic*, *Parenting Teens with Love and Logic*, and even *Grandparenting with Love and Logic*. The authors, Cline and Fay, give great tips and practical suggestions for what to do when a variety of things come up with every age of child. We have found their method of discipline to be effective with thousands of families over the years. Love and logic truly do work. And they especially work with consistency.

Lie #5: Something is wrong with my child.

My parents divorced when I was twenty-two and my little sister was six. That first Christmas, my mom anticipated it being really hard for my six-year-old sister. So she decided to get her a puppy—something I wholeheartedly recommend as both a counselor and dog lover. Over Thanksgiving, my mom and I drove to a little town near our home to look at the puppy. There were only two dogs in the litter, and one couldn't stop following me. "You need to get her this one, Mom. She's got the most personality. And put her in a box under the Christmas tree. I always wanted a puppy in a box under the tree."

So, you may have guessed it already. Christmas morning, in a box under the tree, were two white, teeny Maltese puppies with matching bows and a sign that said, "Sisters for the sisters. The big one is for Sissy, and the little one is for Kathleen." And that is the backstory on my first child—er, puppy—Noel. I tell you to help you understand why this little white furball had such a hold on my heart and why the following incident pulled at everything parental in me.

Noel went to work with me and helped counsel kids every day of her life. At the age of thirteen, she lost her eyesight. She had surgery, mostly because I wasn't ready to let go when the rest of her little body was healthy and whole. Two years later, I was with a group of friends at the beach, and Noel became very sick. She stopped eating one morning and, by lunchtime, would barely lift her head. Early that evening, she started making this sound that was as close to a human scream as I could imagine a dog making. Not long after, I was on the road, in the fog, with Melissa driving Noel and me to the nearest emergency vet, which happened to be an hour and a half away. Noel continued to scream. Honestly, I couldn't take it. Every time she made the sound, I made one equally as loud. I was sobbing. "You're going to be OK; it's going to be OK! Please, Lord, make her feel better! I'm not ready to lose her!" All of it out loud. I was very thankful it was just Noel, Melissa (who happens to be my best friend, so no embarrassment there), and me in the car. Ten minutes away from the vet, she stopped. She laid her head down and relaxed. She was fine.

Turns out, Noel had gas. That's right. Gas from a piece of bacon one of my friends gave her that morning. Who knew gas would make a little dog sound as if she was being tortured? But it did. And I was being tortured right alongside her.

My guess is, as a parent, you have felt something similar but exponentially more. Your child suffers and you suffer. Your daughter is left out of the birthday party for someone she thought was a good friend. Your son is diagnosed with type 1 diabetes. She misses the game-winning goal. He fails another test when you know he tried his best. When you are a parent, your heart is inextricably linked with the heart of your child. To some degree, you feel whatever he or she feels.

When your child feels loss, when he's left out, when she's hurt or she fails, you experience those events right alongside your child. When she or he is diagnosed with something, whether it's a disease, ADD, or depression, you feel the weight of the diagnosis as well. "Something is wrong with my child." Whether it is physical or emotional doesn't really matter. It can easily cause you to lose hope . . . for yourself and for this little one whom you love.

When Noel was making that humanlike sound, if someone had quoted to me Romans 5, I would have honestly wanted to strangle him. But I'm going to quote it to you:

Not only so, but we also glory in our sufferings, because we know that suffering produces perseverance; perseverance, character; and character, hope. And hope does not put us to shame, because God's love has been poured out into our hearts through the Holy Spirit, who has been given to us. (Rom. 5:3–5 NIV)

Suffering produces perseverance. Perseverance produces character. And character produces hope. My guess is that you want your child to have perseverance, character, and hope. It would be nice to skip the suffering. But once again, if you've done more than drive your newborn child home from the hospital, you know you can't skip it. Kids will hurt. They will feel loss and rejection and betrayal. And they may even really have something wrong with them. But after nineteen years of counseling children of all ages, I can honestly say that I believe this verse with every part of who I am. I have seen kids who have suffered more than any child should ever have to suffer. And I have seen, on more occasions than I could name, those very kids be the ones to offer hope—the hope that they have experienced—to other kids who are struggling.

Several years ago, I spoke at a conference for single parents. I brought a group of five teenagers, all with divorced parents, to sit on a panel to answer questions. The first parent to ask a question said, "What do each of you wish your parents had done differently?" Every teenager on the panel—all five—started their answer with some form of the sentence, "Well, I have to say first, if my parents hadn't gotten divorced, I wouldn't be the person I am today." Then they each went on to talk about how difficult it had been then, but how they saw good things in their lives now, as a result.

Truth #5: Suffering produces good things. Even in your child.

People often say that kids are resilient, but I don't believe they are born that way. Resilience is born out of suffering. Resilience is created when kids struggle and learn that they can get through, even overcome, whatever challenge they are facing.

A mom once brought her teenage daughter in for counseling. In our initial session, the mom told me she, herself, had multiple sclerosis and her husband had pancreatic cancer. Her only daughter had just been diagnosed with Asperger's syndrome. "I'm not telling her," this mom quietly said. "The life of our family has been defined by illness, and I'm not going to let illness define her. She will have to deal with it, but I would never want her to allow it to be an excuse."

This young woman is now grown up and finishing her residency in child psychiatry. She is strong and has learned to overcome the social struggles that come with her now-known diagnosis. She is a fighter and learned to fight because of the blows that came against her growing up.

God redeems our struggles. My guess is that you believe that for yourself. But again, it is much harder to believe when you are watching your child suffer. Yet He does and will redeem every bit of suffering in the life of your child. That is the nature of who He is. He has poured out His love for us. That is why we have hope.

I do think it's noteworthy that it doesn't say we produce any of those wonderful things listed in Romans 5. One just leads to the next. And they all end in hope. Hope does not disappoint us. It won't disappoint your son or daughter. He can have hope. She can have hope. You can have hope because of Christ. And sometimes He is the only reason we do.

Something may be wrong with your child, but as I remind parents on an almost-daily basis, Jesus loves your children more than you could ever imagine loving them yourself. He knew every struggle they would face. And He will not only be with them in the midst of their struggles but also turn their struggles into His—and their—good.

Lie #6: I don't have what it takes.

Hopelessness, for all of us, involves the belief at some level that we don't have what it takes. As a parent, you will discover that it's a lie that can wield some serious power.

"If only _____ was my child's mom. She'd know what to do."

"I just read all of this stuff about being strong. I'm not strong enough to handle my son."

I'm not kind enough . . . patient enough . . . fun enough. We could go back to the fill-in-the-blank exercise from the beginning of the chapter. You probably already fill in those blanks plenty. But the very important truth is this:

Truth #6: You have everything that you need.

You were chosen by God to be the parent of your child. We already said that He knew every struggle your child would face. He knew every struggle you would face too. He knew you wouldn't feel that you were enough. But you are.

In Scripture, Queen Esther was credited with not only saving the king but also saving the entire Jewish race. When Esther questioned her ability to carry out her calling, her cousin Mordecai responded by saying, "Who knows but that you have come to your royal position for such a time as this?" (Esther 4:14 NIV).

We don't know what kind of time you're in the midst of as you read this chapter. But, if you've chosen this chapter out of all of the others, there is probably a reason. You feel hopeless and you possibly feel inadequate. Every parent does, at one time or another.

Which of these lies are you most prone to believing?

How does your parenting change when you're living in the midst of the lie?

What truth do you particularly need to hear and remember?

Who and what could serve as reminders for you in this season of parenting?

You may be questioning your calling in the life of your child. You are worried you aren't enough. But God chose you. And He has given you every strength and every characteristic you need to parent your son or daughter. He is the one who produces them anyway. Not you. Not me. He has poured out His love into our hearts. And He has poured out all that you need for such a time as this, whatever time you're facing in the moment.

A Few Hopeful Things to Remember

BOSS YOURSELF BACK. We started off this chapter talking about anxious little Allie. To learn better how to help her, I recently read a book called *Freeing Your Child from Anxiety*. One of the principles the author suggests teaching to children is the ability to boss themselves back. I especially like this idea in my work with little girls, who can tend a little toward bossiness. I help them use that voice and the strength they would use to boss someone else, to boss back their worries.

Let's use Allie as an example. She could boss herself back by saying, "You're silly, Allie. My mom goes to McDonald's because she likes Diet Coke and wants one for herself. Just because we ate there wouldn't mean we'd get fat and die. And I know my mom cares about my nutrition. She makes me eat vegetables way too much not to!"

In essence, that bossing-back idea is why I've based this chapter around the lies we tell ourselves and the truths to combat them. I want you to learn to boss yourself back. When a specific lie comes up, I want you to be able to say, "That's silly, Susan. You have everything it takes to handle Josh right now, because God has chosen you for such a time as this." I want you to remember the truths yourself. I want you to share the lies you're most vulnerable to with your spouse and/or closest friends. Tell them the truths, too, and let them use their bossy voices to bring you back to truth.

HAVE LIFE AND HOPE OUTSIDE OF YOUR CHILDREN AND THEIR CIRCUMSTANCES. In Melissa's and my book *Modern Parents, Vintage Values*, we talk about Romans 5. We said that hope will not disappoint you, but your child will. You need interests outside of your son and daughter. Take an art class. Go on trips with friends. Take time for dinner dates with your spouse. Have things you enjoy that are separate from your children. Those things will help you come back to them refreshed and remind you that there is a bigger picture. Yes, your heart is interconnected with the heart of your child. But you are still you. And they need you to be. They need you to have hope outside of them. And ultimately, any real hope comes from the fact that God has poured out His love into our hearts—and theirs.

REMEMBER THAT YOU AND THEY ARE A WORK IN PROGRESS. When I was thirty-six, I went to a seminar by an author I greatly respect, Richard Rohr. He said that we become our real selves at the age of thirty-six. Ironic, huh? I don't know that I had become my real self at that point, but I hope I'm in the process. And I know that however close or far from thirty-six you are, you're in the same process. He said we become our real selves when we realize two things:

1. Life doesn't work the way we thought it would.
2. We don't work the way we think we should.

Kind of sounds like the point is that nothing works. And that could leave you just as hopeless at the end of this chapter as you were at the beginning. But that is definitely not the point—not mine nor, I think, his. The point is that you are free when you realize those two things; you are free to give up the idea that your child has to keep up, or you're supposed to be some kind of parent that you're not. You're free to love and enjoy your child without all of the "supposed to's" that can cause you to be discouraged and hopeless in the first place. In essence, you're free to be the parent God has called you to be. And in that freedom, you can have hope enough to get through whatever lies you or your child might face.

12.

Being a Free Parent

—with Melissa

BLUEBERRY HAS COST ME A LOT OF MONEY IN the last few months. We've been in dog obedience school. And, boy, do I mean *we*. We're now on our second dog trainer. Our first dog trainer was very disciplined. He could flatten his hand in a downward motion, and his dog would lie down one hundred yards away. Blueberry . . . not so much. She and I both have a hard time remembering which command goes with which hand motion and what it's all supposed to mean. I tell her, "Down," and she tries to shake. I tell her to sit, and she puts her front paws on my shoulders to try to hug me. It's all very confusing. But there's one command that has been particularly mysterious to both of us, especially as I've written this chapter.

"Free."

The first trainer told me that after Blueberry has been "in a down" or "in a sit" for a given period of time, I'm supposed to say, "Free." When I first said it, Blueberry just looked at me. She tilted her head in a "What in the world does that mean?" kind of way. I didn't know either. We both just shrugged.

Now she's getting the hang of it. I think she's partly getting the hang of it because of our new trainer. She is more of a positive reinforcement than negative reinforcement–type of trainer. She took away the "obedience" collar Blueberry wore and replaced it with treats. One trip from Nashville to Kentucky in the car necessitates an entire bag of treats. I think, though, it's helped Blueberry feel more loved. And more secure. And it's given her more confidence in what *free* truly means. When I say, "Free," Blueberry now knows that she can run and play, or find her ball, or give me a hug, or whatever she wants to do. She is free because she is loved and secure and is no longer afraid of punishment.

I think I'm a lot like Blueberry. When I first started working on this chapter, I was perplexed. Free? What does that mean in terms of parenting? Sissy and David wanted me to be the one to write this chapter because of something I said in a conference—that instead of focusing on being the parent God's called you to be, you can focus on being the parent God frees you to be. It sounds good. But I really wasn't even sure what I meant at the time.

After studying this idea of freedom, I think I know a lot more now. And that's basically that I'm free. Like Blueberry, I'm free to love and laugh and dance and teach and counsel and write, because I'm loved. I'm also free to discipline. You are, too, as a parent. But so often we live with the confusion that Blueberry and I did. We turn our heads, shrug our shoulders, and stay in the sit position for entirely too long.

Let me give another example, and one that involves a human child rather than a furry one. You need a little background first, though. I attend an Anglican church. It's one of the more progressive Anglican churches, where they intersperse hymns with worship choruses. Church members are very engaged in the service, although there isn't a ton of outward expression. Suffice it to say most people are not waving flags and dancing in the aisles. Most. So on this particular day, I was sitting in my pew toward the back of the church. It was the last song of the service, which usually is a rousing, anthemic song, such as "In Christ Alone" or "Mighty to Save." Most of the church was on their feet . . . on their feet in their pews, I should say. But there was a ten-year-old girl toward the front of the church who was just not having the stuffy standing around any longer. She was out, in the aisle, dancing freely. I watched her for a few minutes, and then saw a woman I guessed was her mom quickly moving toward her from the back of the church. *Uh-oh*, I thought. *That's not going to last long.* Her mom walked up to her daughter, took her hand, and then—it was as if I watched this moment pass over the mom's face—started dancing too.

Free.

I have to admit that I was shocked. I fully expected that mother to put her daughter right back in the pew. But maybe that's because I'm not very free myself. I think, in that moment, the mother made a decision. "Should I make her sit in the pew beside me, or should I join in her worship? Is it more important to not look foolish in front of people, or to respond to what I feel stirring inside me with my daughter? Does it matter to me what they think? Do I really feel free?"

It could have gone either way. It could have been that the mother saw her daughter's dance as an attempt to get attention. She could have been embarrassed for her daughter and embarrassed for herself. But in that moment, she chose to believe and act on something different.

Free.

As a parent, this chapter may be one of the most difficult to live out. You may be more like Blueberry and me. Free? What is that supposed to mean? I have to have a healthy dinner on the table by six o'clock, make sure my son is ready for his spelling test, plan the perfect party for my daughter's tenth birthday, call my mother, walk the dog, exercise, and spend the few minutes left over with my husband. How can you be free in the midst of that much pressure?

The Parent Pressure Trap

What kind of pressure are you feeling right now? The pressure to be a good parent? The pressure to make sure your child turns out godly and well-rounded? The pressure to be intentional, even? You could close this book feeling more pressure to be intentional, patient, balanced, spiritual, and a whole host of other things you hadn't even thought about before you picked it up. But if you did, you would have missed the point.

We want you to be free.

This book is not called *Effective Parenting.* It is not called the *7 Secrets of Highly Successful Moms or Dads.* It's not called *Raising a Perfect Child, Being a Perfect Parent.* It's not called *Doing It Right: How to Make Your Child Turn Out Good.* There is no "right" in parenting. There's no "highly successful" or "perfect" for parents or children. There is not a model, perfect family . . . even in the Bible. Words such as *perfect, successful,* and *right* just serve to create more pressure. We live in a pressure-producing, results-oriented society.

As a parent, the pressure is on you . . . and the results of your parenting are on display in your child's behavior. If you're a good parent, your child will turn out well. If you are a godly parent, your child will have a strong faith throughout his growing up. If you raise her with good manners, she'll act appropriately. If you teach him well about character, he'll grow up with a compassionate heart and generous spirit. If you spend enough time with your daughter, she'll be confident.

If . . . then. We could call those two words the Parent Pressure Trap. If you do this, then that happens. We all fall into it at times. We believe that if we would only pray for our kids enough, or have consistent family devotions, or send our children to the right school, or say the right thing in a given situation, then our kids would turn out the way we hope. We would get the desired results. But, we don't. We don't do it perfectly, and even on those rare occasions when we do, things don't turn out the way we imagined. The if-then theory doesn't work. It actually breaks down at several points along the ellipses.

The first problem is *you.* You can't be a perfect parent. You will not be godly in all of your decisions. You will fail, and fail often, as you raise your child. To live under the pressure of trying to be a perfect parent only creates guilt. Leslie Leyland Fields said, "I know now that parenting is not meant to paralyze me with guilt but to send me running freely to God. Parenting is not meant to cripple me with insufficiency but to lead me to God's sufficiency. Parenting is so much less about me and so much more about God!"[1]

Fields's quote unveils the second problem in our theory. Parenting is really not about you. In other words, you are not in control. Even if you could, for a few moments, be a perfect parent, you could not create the desired outcome in your child. You can't directly change your child's heart . . . or behavior. You can be intentional, but you can't assuredly be effective. When you believe that your behavior can produce the desired results, you put pressure on yourself that God never intended you to feel.

In his book *The Pressure's Off*, Larry Crabb asserts, "The illusion of control brings requirement, requirement creates pressure, pressure leads to slavery, the slavery of having to figure out life to make it work. Those who hold on to the illusion of control lose the enjoyment of freedom."[2]

We're back to that word again. Free.

But to get there, we've first got to get rid of the pressure. How? We believe it's in letting go of the illusion of control. For example, it is not in your power to raise a godly child. Just because you pray with him every night, attend church regularly, make him memorize scripture, and have weekly family devotionals does not guarantee that your son will be godly by age fourteen. It's not in your control to make him a godly child. Doing everything right doesn't work. But, oh, how we want it to. Of course we do. And that is where we get into trouble. We start to focus on the results, rather than on God. We want godly kids, rather than to be godly parents, or even just to know God better. Parenting is so much less about me and so much more about God.

Where are you making your parenting about you?

Where do you feel pressure?

What are the if-then's in your life today?

What would it mean for you to let go of the illusion of control?

How could you trust the outcome to God?

"The former regulation is set aside because it was weak and useless (for the law made nothing perfect), and a better hope is introduced, by which we draw near to God" (Heb. 7:18–19 NIV).

A Better Hope

The spiritual journey is rooted in liberty, the freedom of grace: come as you are, trembling, and learn to rest. Then go out into life doing what's right because you're privileged to do so, because you want to be holy, not because doing right is the way to a pleasant life.[3]

Trying to constantly do it right leads to pressure. It is, in effect, living under the laws of if-then. Liberty, grace, and rest sure sound better than pressure and laws, don't they? The good news is that the pressure *is* off. We *can* rest. But we can only learn to rest when we give up the illusion of control. In other words, when we trust in God rather than our frustrated attempts at perfect parenting. We can and are privileged to live this free life because of Christ. But, oh, how quickly we forget.

The Galatians forgot too. They knew that Jesus had come to fulfill the law. They no longer had to. But by the time Paul wrote his letter to them, they had fallen back into their old ways. Maybe they were expecting some kind of desired outcome. Maybe they had started to believe the if–thens of their day. Either way, I would guess they were feeling pressure. But Paul wanted to remind them—to beg them—to immerse themselves in the better hope, which is Jesus.

> Christ has set us free to live a free life. So take your stand! Never again let anyone put a harness of slavery on you. . . .
>
> It is absolutely clear that God has called you to a free life. Just make sure that you don't use this freedom as an excuse to do whatever you want to do and destroy your freedom. Rather, use your freedom to serve one another in love; that's how freedom grows. For everything we know about God's Word is summed up in a single sentence: Love others as you love yourself. That's an act of true freedom. (Gal. 5:1, 13–15 MSG)

Parenting Freely

The three of us lost a friend this year who fought a valiant battle against a brain tumor. Her name was Marky. She was an artistic, courageous, exceedingly kind single mom of two grown daughters. Her life had been quite a journey, fraught with sadness and joy, pain and lots of laughter. When she died, her daughters

dressed her in her favorite outfit—shorts, sandals, and a T-shirt
that aptly read "More Blessed Than Stressed."

You can be free, as a person and as a parent, no matter how
much pressure you feel today. You can't do it right. You can't be
the perfect parent, and you can't create the desired outcome in
your child. But you can immerse yourself in the better hope that
Hebrews 7 speaks of. You can fix your eyes on Jesus. You can
entrust your child to Him. He's really the one in control, anyway.
And He loves you both more than you could ask or imagine.

> But when the time arrived that was set by God the Father,
> God sent his Son, born among us of a woman, born under
> the conditions [pressure] of the law so that he might redeem
> those of us who have been kidnapped by the law. Thus we
> have been set free to experience our rightful heritage. You
> can tell for sure that you are now fully adopted as his own
> children because God sent the Spirit of his Son into our lives
> crying out, "Papa! Father!" Doesn't that privilege of intimate
> conversation with God make it plain that you are not a slave,
> but a child? (Gal. 4:4–7 MSG)

You are set free, because of the great love your Father has for
you both. You are free to take your daughter's hand and dance
with her in the aisle. You are free to be an intentional parent. You
are free to be balanced and connected and consistent and merciful too. We love because God first loved us. And you are free to
be the parent God has freed you to be, because He has been all
of those things with you first.

Maybe you can go on autopilot, after all.

Free.

Notes

Chapter 1: Being an Intentional Parent

1. Dan Allender, *How Children Raise Parents: The Art of Listening to Your Family* (Colorado Springs: WaterBrook Press, 2003), xii.
2. Anne Lamott, *Traveling Mercies: Some Thoughts on Faith* (New York: Random House, 1999), 131.
3. Donald Miller, *A Million Miles in a Thousand Years* (Nashville: Thomas Nelson, 2009), xiii, 248.

Chapter 2: Being a Patient Parent

1. "How to Be Patient," wikiHow, http://www.wikihow.com/Be-Patient, accessed February 25, 2012.
2. Dictionary.com, s.v. "Passion," http://dictionary.reference.com/browse/passion, accessed February 26, 2012.
3. Melissa Trevathan and Sissy Goff, *Modern Parents, Vintage Values* (Nashville: B&H Publishing, 2010), 259.
4. *Wikipedia*, s.v. "Frontal Lobe," http://en.wikipedia.org/wiki/Frontal_lobe, accessed February 26, 2012.

5. "Frontal Lobes," Centre for NeuroSkills, http://www
.neuroskills.com/brain-injury/frontal-lobes.php, accessed
February 26, 2012.

Chapter 3: Being a Grown-Up Parent

1. Warren Roberts, Charles T. Boulton, and Elizabeth Mansfield, eds., *The Letters of D. H. Lawrence* (Cambridge: Cambridge University Press, 2002), 48.
2. J. M. Barrie, *Margaret Ogilvy, by Her Son, J. M. Barrie* (New York: Charles Scribner's Sons, 1923), 30.
3. *Urban Dictionary*, s.v. "Hipster," http://www.urbandictionary .com/define.php?term=hipster, accessed May 14, 2012.
4. Christine Rosen, "The Hipster Curse: The Parents Who Don't Want to Be Adults," http://www.catholiceducation.org/articles /parenting/pa0146.htm, accessed May 14, 2012.
5. Anne Lamott, *Plan B* (New York: Riverhead Books, 2005), 102.
6. J. R. R. Tolkien, "On Fairy-Stories," *The Tolkien Reader* (New York: Ballantine Books, 1966), 44–45.

Chapter 4: Being a Balanced Parent

1. Gina Bria, *The Art of Family* (New York: Dell, 1998), 162–63.

Chapter 5: Being a Consistent Parent

1. Aldous Huxley, *Do What You Will* (London: Chatto & Windus, 1931), 125.
2. Melissa Trevathan, and Sissy Goff, *Modern Parents, Vintage Values* (Nashville: B&H Publishing Group, 2010), 153–54.
3. Stephen James and David Thomas, *Wild Things* (Carol Stream, IL: Tyndale House Publishers, 2009), 27.
4. Melissa Trevathan and Sissy Goff, *Raising Girls* (Grand Rapids: Zondervan, 2007), 61.
5. Dorothy G. Singer and Tracey A. Revenson, *A Piaget Primer: How a Child Thinks* (New York: Penguin Group: 1978), 128.
6. Melissa Trevathan and Sissy Goff, *The Back Door to Your Teen's Heart* (Eugene, OR: Harvest House, 2002), 15.

7. Melissa Trevathan and Sissy Goff, *Raising Girls* (Grand Rapids: Zondervan, 2007), 68.
8. "Teaching Young Children Responsibility," Education.com, http://www.education.com/reference/article/Ref_Teaching_2/.
9. Foster Cline and Jim Fay, *Parenting Teens with Love and Logic* (Colorado Springs: Pinon Press, 1992, 2006), 49.
10. Jim Fay and Charles Fay, *Love and Logic Magic for Early Childhood* (Golden, CO: Love and Logic Institute, 2000), 71.
11. Cline and Fay, *Parenting Teens with Love and Logic*, 28.
12. Walter Wangerin, *Little Lamb, Who Made Thee?* (New York: HarperCollins, 1993), 69.

Chapter 6: Being a Playful Parent
1. Louise Boynton, *Century Magazine*, December 1906.
2. Amelia Hill, "Parents are forgetting how to play with their children, study shows," Guardian.co.uk, August 26, 2010.
3. Dan Allender, *How Children Raise Parents* (Colorado Springs: WaterBrook Press, 2003), 202.
4. Stuart Brown with Christopher Vaughan, *Play: How It Shapes the Brain, Opens the Imagination, and Invigorates the Soul* (New York: Penguin Group, 2009), 127.
5. Terry Lindvall, *Surprised by Laughter* (Nashville: Thomas Nelson Publishers, 1996), 111.
6. Johann Wolfgang von Goethe, *Maxims and Reflections* (Seattle: Createspace, 2011), 39.

Chapter 8: Being an Encouraging Parent
1. Helen Granat, *Wisdom Through the Ages*, bk. 2 (Victoria, BC: Trafford Publishing, 2003), 93.
2. Larry Crabb and Dan Allender, *Encouragement* (Grand Rapids: Zondervan, 1984), 80.
3. Ibid., 71.
4. Frederick Buechner, *Whistling in the Dark* (San Francisco: HarperCollins, 1988), xi.
5. Donald Miller, *Blue Like Jazz* (Nashville: Thomas Nelson, 2003), 220.

6. "Understanding Depression," KidsHealth, http://kidshealth
.org/parent/emotions/feelings/understanding_depression.html,
accessed May 6, 2012.
7. Tamar E. Chansky, *Freeing your Child from Anxiety* (New York:
Broadway Books, 2004), 3.
8. James Burns, "Bullying Statistics," Proactive Behaviorial
Management, http://behavioral-management.com
/bullying-statistics, accessed May 6, 2012.
9. Kelly Corrigan, *The Middle Place* (New York: Hyperion, 2008), 4.

Chapter 9: Being a Spiritual Parent
1. Leslie Leyland Fields, *Parenting Is Your Highest Calling*
(Colorado Springs: WaterBrook Press, 2008), 149.
2. Eugene Peterson, *Like Dew Your Youth* (Grand Rapids: Wm. B.
Eerdmans Publishing Co., 1976), 10.
3. Madeline L'Engle, "Word," *The Weather of the Heart* (Wheaton,
IL: H. Shaw, 1978, 2001), 52.

Chapter 10: Being a Merciful Parent
1. ThinkExist.com Quotations, http://thinkexist.com/quotations
/making_the_decision_to_have_a_child_is_
momentous/204463.html.

Chapter 11: Being a Hopeful Parent
1. Anne Lamott, *Plan B* (New York: Riverhead Books, 2005), 94.

Chapter 12: Being a Free Parent
1. Leslie Leyland Fields, *Parenting Is Your Highest Calling*
(Colorado Springs: WaterBrook Press, 2008), 284.
2. Larry Crabb, *The Pressure's Off* (Colorado Springs: WaterBrook
Press, 2002), 7.
3. Ibid, 26.

Acknowledgments

THANK YOU, MATT BAUGHER, FOR BELIEVING IN the three of us, and for being so excited to bring us on board. Thank you, as well, to the team at Thomas Nelson for welcoming us in such a warm way.

We have much gratitude for David and Amy Huffman, and the many ways you support us, as our agents, managers, and friends.

We continue to be grateful to work alongside so many wonderful folks at Daystar. What a rare gift it is to genuinely enjoy the folks you work with as much as we do.

It makes it easier to write about this subject when you are surrounded by many friends and family members who are so intentional. We remain thankful for the many people who enrich our lives.

About the Authors

SISSY GOFF, MEd, LPC-MHSP, is the counseling director for children and adolescents at Daystar. The author of five books, she is a frequent radio guest and contributor to magazines. Sissy has a master's degree from Vanderbilt University and is a sought-after speaker for parenting and teacher training events.

DAVID THOMAS, LMSW, is the counseling director for men and boys at Daystar. A popular speaker and the coauthor of five books, he is a frequent guest on national television and radio, and a regular contributor to *ParentLife* magazine. David and his wife, Connie, have a daughter and twin sons.

MELISSA TREVATHAN, MRE, is founder and executive director of Daystar Counseling Ministries. A graduate of Southwestern Baptist Seminary, Melissa has taught graduate courses, spoken to various churches and schools across the country, and been a guest on television and radio programs throughout the US and Canada. She is a popular speaker for parents, teachers, and kids of all ages.